LANGUAGE
Fundamentals Vol. 1

The Nuts and Bolts of Written Language

Language Fundamentals contains materials suitable for students working at a grade one through grade three level. This broad range is included to meet the needs of students at diverse ability levels in the same classroom. This volume is especially helpful if you have a combination or multi-age class. Materials are designed for the practice of language skills. You can select the practice pages needed by your whole class, a small group, or an individual child. The pages can also be used for homework practice.

Table of Contents

Congratulations on your purchase of some of the finest teaching materials in the world.

Entire contents copyright ©1995 by EVAN-MOOR CORP.
18 Lower Ragsdale Drive, Monterey, CA 93940-5746

Permission is hereby granted to the individual purchaser to reproduce student materials in this book for non-commercial individual or classroom use only. Permission is not granted for school-wide, or system-wide, reproduction of materials.

Author: Jo Ellen Moore
Illustrator: Rick Law
Editor: Joy Evans
Cover: Cheryl Kashata

Evan-Moor
EDUCATIONAL PUBLISHERS

The **Answer Key** for this section
is found on pages 55-56.

Section
One

Mechanics

What do we mean by "mechanics"?

Mechanics is the basic "nuts and bolts" of written language. It is recognizing what makes a sentence complete, knowing how to punctuate the sentence, and knowing where to put capital letters.

What is included in this section?

- Sentences *(pages 4-11)*
    - -recognizing when a group of words creates a complete thought
    - -identifying statements, questions, commands, and exclamations
- Capitalization *(pages 12-28)*:
    - -recognizing capital letters
    - -using capital letters:
        - at the beginning of a sentence
        - in proper nouns
        - in titles
- Punctuation *(page 29)*:
    - -recognizing when to use:
        - periods
        - question marks
        - exclamation points
        - commas
        - quotation marks
    - -using correct punctuation when writing one's own sentences

Using the pages in this section:

When selecting pages to use with your students, consider which areas they need to practice and at what level that practice needs to be. The variety of pages available for use allows you to individualize practice activities to better meet your students' needs.

At the simplest level there are pages asking children to identify whether something is a sentence or not and to add a capital and a period.

At the highest level there are pages requiring students to determine whether a sentence is a statement, a command, an exclamation, or a question and to use correct punctuation, including commas and quotation marks.

Sentences

The student:
- recognizes when a group of words creates a complete thought
- identifies statements, questions, commands, and exclamations

The dog sat down.

a brown bone

"Whole or Part?"
Write phrases and sentences on sentences strips. Have children read the strips and determine which are the sentences.

"Building Sentences"
Make subject and predicate strips to practice building sentences. Place the subject strips where the children with whom you are working can see them. Pass out the predicate strips. Have each child come up and place his/her strip with a subject to make a complete sentence. Collect the cards and reverse the process.

All the bugs

sat on a leaf.

"Ask Me - Tell Me"
Have a small group of children sit with the teacher. Place two paper lunch bags in front of you. Make a question mark and the word "ask" on one bag. Make a period and the work "tell" on the other. Place small objects in each bag. (Model the following activity before you ask your students to do it.)

Call a child up to select an object out of either bag. If the object is from the "tell" bag, the child makes a statement about it using a complete sentence. (For example, if the child takes an eraser from the bag, he/she might say "This is a big pink eraser" or "You use an eraser to correct mistakes in writing.") If the object is from the "ask" bag, the child asks a question. (For example, "What color is this eraser?" or "Do you know how to use an eraser?")

After making a question or statement, the child puts the object into the opposite bag so that if it's taken from the bag by the next child, the same statement or question isn't reused. Continue until all students in the group have one or more turns.

"What Do You See Here?"
Show a picture to the group. Call on one child at a time and ask "What do you see here?" Listen for use of complete sentences. You may also tape the picture to a sheet of chart paper and write the complete sentences used by your students.

Subject and Predicate

1. Cut out the strips.
2. Paste them to make sentences.

Bob and Amy	paste
My funny little puppy	paste
On Sunday morning, Mr. Brown	paste
All the circus elephants	paste
The students in Room 5	paste

are my pet kittens.

likes to play with his rubber bone.

cooks breakfast for his wife.

marched down the street.

are going on a class trip.

Find the Sentences

A sentence tells who or what did something and what was done.

Put a circle around the sentences:

1. In the tub.

2. Nan came to see me.

3. He is a big man.

4. At lunch.

5. The cat had a nap.

6. A red can.

7. Sam has a dog.

8. His dog can get the ball.

9. On the box.

How many did you find?

Sentence Search

Circle each complete sentence.

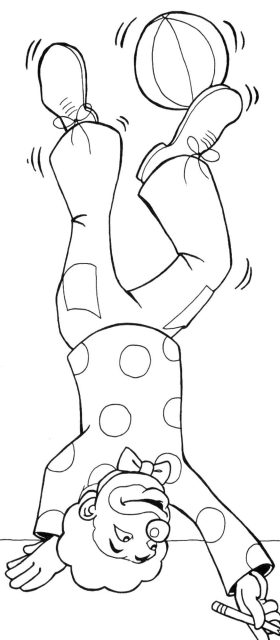

1. In the sandbox.

2. Across the street.

3. She went into the store.

4. My best friend.

5. This is a pretty hat.

6. Do you want some ice cream?

7. On Monday morning.

8. At 6:00.

9. The clown did a funny trick.

10. Sam flew his airplane.

11. This red bird.

12. Let's paint the house green.

13. His dog played ball.

14. In my pocket.

15. Put your coat on that chair.

How many sentences did you find?

Good for you!

Sentence Sleuth

Circle each complete sentence.

1. The bear ate five big fish.

2. One sunny day.

3. To play ball.

4. Down the street.

5. The yellow kitten climbed a tree.

6. A little boy ran.

7. Betty and Sam.

8. Under the red and white blanket.

9. Six birds flew.

10. To catch the mice.

11. See that funny.

12. Quick as a wink.

13. Will you come to my house?

14. Mother called the boys.

15. Let's go now.

How many sentences did you find? ☐ Good for you!

A Complete Sentence

A complete sentence must name a person, place, or thing and then tell what happens.
A complete sentence begins with a capital letter and ends with a punctuation mark.

> ## The monkeys played in the trees.

Read the groups of words below.
Draw a circle around the complete sentences.

1. Running through the park with the dog.

2. Toby ran as fast as he could.

3. Kim and her friends.

4. The team won their game.

5. The friendly cat.

6. The gorilla ate a banana.

7. Jerome flew down the road on his skates.

8. Under the table.

9. His bike has a flat tire.

10. Did you see the little kitten?

11. In the blue car.

12. Down the hill.

13. Bob went to get a toy.

14. A bee sat on his hat.

15. Stop the wagon.

©1995 by Evan-Moor Corp.   Language Fundamentals

Find a Match

Match to make a sentence.

Sam and George   flew over my house.

The school bus   looked for fruit to eat.

A trail of ants   had a flat tire.

Invaders from space   were best friends.

The band of gorillas   crawled into the picnic basket.

A helicopter   landed in the park last night.

Pick one sentence. Draw a picture about it here.

Tell About It

Write three sentences about this picture.

_____

_ _

1. _____

_____

_ _

_____

_ _

2. _____

_____

_ _

_____

_ _

3. _____

_____

_ _

_____

Capital Letters

The student:
• uses a capital letter at the beginning of sentences
• uses captial letters to start:
-names of people
-days of week
-months of the year
-place names
-titles

Match the Letter
Make a set of alphabet cards for both upper and lower case letters (pages 13-18). Give students five or more pairs (A a) and ask them to match the capital with the lower case letter. Put the cards in an envelope and put them in a center for independent practice. (This can be done using cursive letters for older students.)

Capital Letters in Names
Put a list of your students' names on the chalkboard. Begin each with a lower case letter. Have children come up and erase the first lower case letter in their own name and write in the capital. Put up your name also and point out that your "title" starts with a capital letter also.

This activity can be repeated with any list of proper nouns.

Green Means Go!
Put sentences on the chalkboard. Begin each sentence with a lower case letter. Have children read the sentences with you. Erase the first letter and replace it with a capital using green chalk. Explain that green stands for "start" or "go" and shows that you are starting a sentence. Explain that a sentence <u>always</u> starts with a capital letter.

W
we learn everyday.

Observe how children use capital letters in their own writings. This will help you determine who needs what type of practice.

Alphabet Matching Cards

Reproduce the cards on pages 13-18 to use with the alphabet matching activity on page 12.

A

B

C

D

E

F

G

H

I	J	K
L	M	N
O	P	Q

R	S	T
U	V	W
X	Y	Z

©1995 by Evan-Moor Corp. Language Fundamentals

a	b	c
d	e	f
g	h	i

©1995 by Evan-Moor Corp.
Language Fundamentals

j	k	l
m	n	o
p	q	r

©1995 by Evan-Moor Corp. Language Fundamentals

s t u

v w x

y z

Capital Letters

Trace.

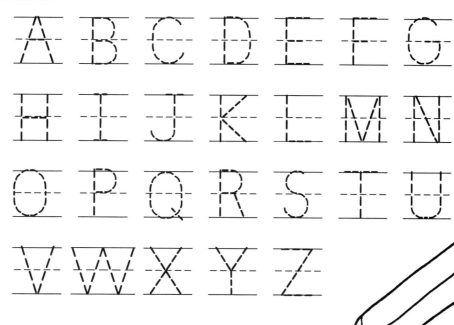

A B C D E F G
H I J K L M N
O P Q R S T U
V W X Y Z

Write.

A

Using Capital Letters

A sentence starts with a capital letter.

Fill in the capital letters with a green crayon.

1. my pet is not big.

2. it cannot run and hop.

3. my pet can swim.

4. it is as yellow as butter.

5. can you tell what my pet is?

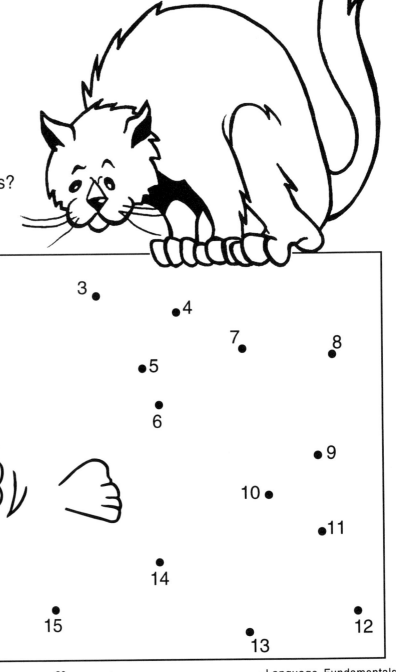

Start at 1. Connect the dots.

3
4
7
8
2
5
6
9
1
10
11
16
14
15
13
12

Capitalization

> **Every sentence begins with a capital letter.**
>
> **T**he ice cream was good.
>
> **M**y mother picked me up at the park.
>
> **W**hat is your name?

Read the sentences.
Circle the words that should have capital letters.

1. the girl was sad when her friend moved away.

2. a cow with black and white spots was eating grass.

3. johnny went to the park to play.

4. saturday was so hot we all went to the beach.

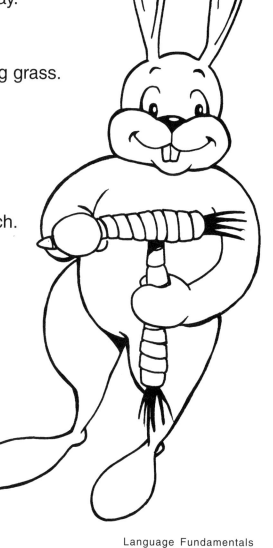

5. does it ever rain in the desert?

6. can you help me with my homework?

7. betty has a new pet snake.

8. how fast can you run around the track?

©1995 by Evan-Moor Corp.   Language Fundamentals

Names Start with Capital Letters

A B C D E F G H I J K L M N O P Q R S T U V W X Y Z

kelly jones

_____

maurice brown

_____

ann lee

_____

carlota toscano

_____

bobby miller

_____

jose contreras

_____

tiffany conners

_____

tony reinhart

_____

sidney feinstein

_____

My name is

_____

Days of the Week

Days of the week start with capital letters.

monday _____

tuesday _____

wednesday _____

thursday _____

friday _____

saturday _____

sunday _____

Today is _____

Place Names

Place names begin with capital letters.

Circle the capital letters.

Brown's Bakery

Washington Elementary School

Fifth Avenue

Yellowstone Park

Pittsburgh, Pennsylvania

Medicine Bow, Alberta

Joe's Quick Cuts

Museum of Natural History

Six Flags Over Texas

Places to Go

Place names begin with capital letters.
Can you write the capital letters for these place names?

new york city

canada

ben's bakery

lake ann

snake river

disneyland

lincoln high school

point reyes

mississippi river

wall street

mount lassen

©1995 by Evan-Moor Corp.

Language Fundamentals

Look for Capitals

Find the words that should be capitalized.
Change the letters.

1. <u>M</u>~~m~~y name is <u>H</u>~~h~~arry <u>H</u>~~h~~opper.

2. can you go to the movies saturday night?

3. marta lives on washington street.

4. i am going to canada on my vacation.

5. does your uncle live in vermont?

6. marshall's birthday is on monday.

7. did mary jo and ben move to toronto?

©1995 by Evan-Moor Corp.

Language Fundamentals

Using Capital Letters

Always use a capital letter with:
- proper nouns and the pronoun *I*
- titles
- days, months, and holidays
- cities, states, and countries

Circle the words in these sentences that need capital letters.
Write the sentences, putting in the capital letters.

1. My cousin, pedro, lives in san diego, california.

2. teresa said, "i am going to texas in july."

3. mrs. brown was born in florida, but now she lives in canada.

4. can you come to my house for easter dinner?

What Is Missing?

Circle the words in these sentences that need capital letters.
Write the sentences, putting in the capital letters.

1. My teacher, (professor) (green,) lives in (dallas,) (texas.)

_____

_____

_____

2. kisha and tamara went to disneyland for a vacation.

_____

_____

_____

3. mr. martin cooked thanksgiving dinner.

_____

_____

_____

4. school will be out at the end of may.

_____

_____

_____

Punctuation

The student:
- recognizes when to use:
  - periods
  - question marks
  - exclamation points
  - commas
  - quotation marks
- uses correct punctuation when writing one's own sentences

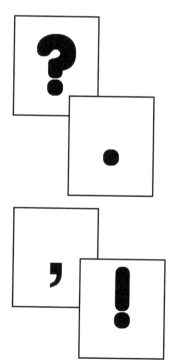

Red Means Stop!
Put sentences on the chalkboard. Have children read the sentences with you. Add a period or question mark at the end of each sentence using red chalk. Explain that red means "stop" and that the punctuation mark at the end of a sentence means "stop - this sentence is over."

Show Me
Make "Show Me" cards (page 31) for each student. These can be a set of cards in an envelope or can be held together by a ring in the corner. The set should include all of the types of punctuation marks you are currently practicing.

Prepare a set of sentences, without punctuation marks, on sentence strips. Show a sentence and read it with your students. Ask students to "Show" the punctuation mark that should go at the end of the sentence. If they are ready to do sentences containing several punctuation marks, point to a place in the sentence and ask "Which punctuation mark goes here?"

**"The time has come," the Walrus said,
"to speak of many things!"**

Tara said, "This lava rock is light."

"I wanted you to see my book about dinosaurs," said Gus.

Is It a Quote?

Select a page containing dialog from a story your children can read. Make a plastic overlay for an overhead projector or make individual copies for children. Have the children underline each sentence of dialog to help them know where to start and when to stop. Have children take the parts of the characters and read aloud only the dialog from a story.

"The Time Has Come to Speak of Many Things"

Set up a sharing center titled "The time has come," the Walrus said, "to speak of many things!" Arrange a table below this board so that children can display objects they've brought to school to share. Provide a supply of tag sentence strips and a black marking pen. Have each child write, or dictate, a sentence about what he/she is sharing. Be sure students who write their own sentences use quotation marks correctly before you place their "quote" in the sharing center.

Observe how children use punctuation marks in their own writing. This will help you determine who needs what type of practice.

period

question
mark

?

.

exclamation
mark

comma

!

,

©1995 by Evan-Moor Corp.
Language Fundamentals

Telling Sentences

A statement tells us something.
We use a period at the end of a statement.

Put a period at the end of each of these statements.

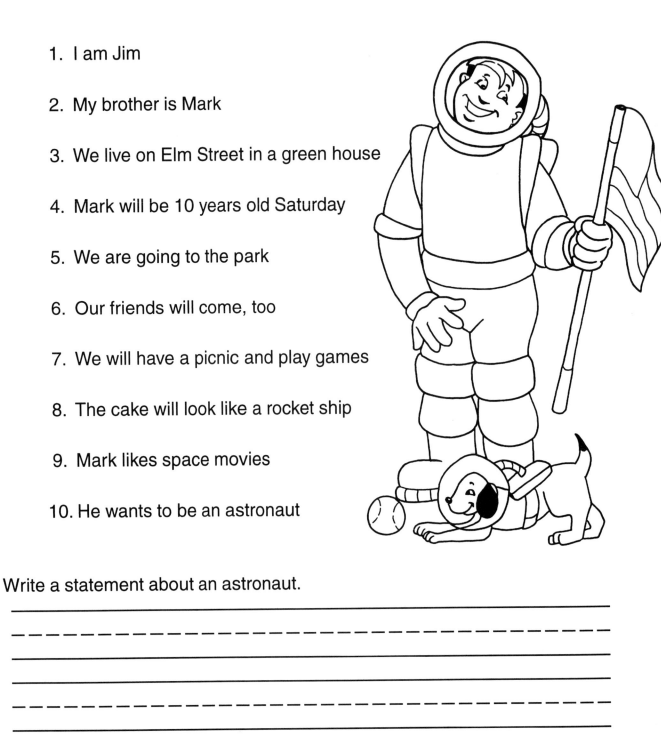

1. I am Jim

2. My brother is Mark

3. We live on Elm Street in a green house

4. Mark will be 10 years old Saturday

5. We are going to the park

6. Our friends will come, too

7. We will have a picnic and play games

8. The cake will look like a rocket ship

9. Mark likes space movies

10. He wants to be an astronaut

Write a statement about an astronaut.

_____

_____

_____

_____

©1995 by Evan-Moor Corp.   Language Fundamentals

Asking Sentences

A question mark is used at the end of
a sentence that asks something.

Put a **?** at the end of these "asking" sentences.

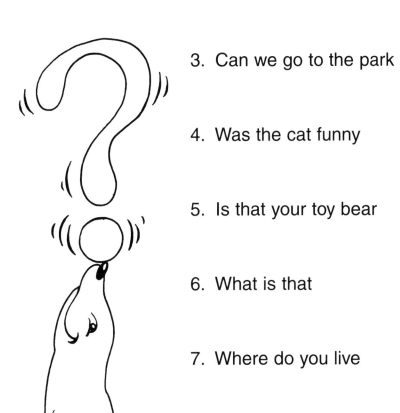

1. Can Bob ride a bike

2. Do you want to go to my house

3. Can we go to the park

4. Was the cat funny

5. Is that your toy bear

6. What is that

7. Where do you live

8. Do you like popcorn

©1995 by Evan-Moor Corp.   Language Fundamentals

Question Marks

We use a **question mark** at the end of a question.
A question asks us something.
Put a question mark at the end of each of these questions.

What is your name

Where do you live

How old are you

Can you jump rope

Do you like to go to the zoo

Have you ever found a lizard in your yard

Would you like pizza for dinner

Shall we go to the pet shop

Which dog would you like to have

Doesn't that puppy have funny ears

Were you here last week

Is that your mother

Write a question about a little monkey.

_____

_____

_____

_____

_____

What Comes at the End?

A **statement** (telling sentence) gets a

A **question** (asking sentence) gets a

Match:

1. Can you play jump rope   .

2. I like to run and hop   .

3. Morris has a pet frog   ?

4. What is in the box   ?

5. Alma has a baby sister   ?

6. Where did it go   .

Period or Question Mark

Put a **period** at the end of each statement.
Put a **question mark** at the end of each question.

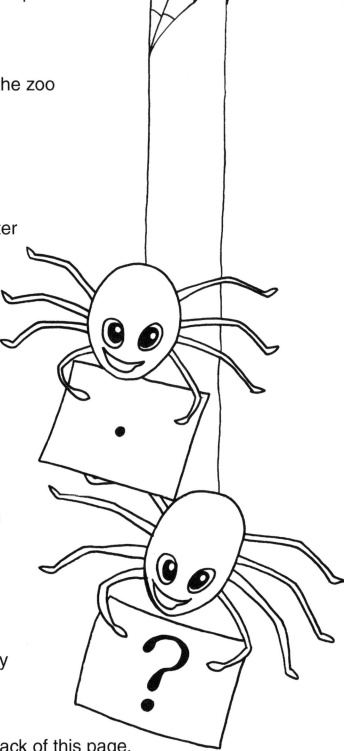

1. Who is going to the zoo with us

2. We will meet Bobby and Carol at the zoo

3. Do you like snakes

4. Gorillas scare me

5. Carol saw a baby hippo in the water

6. Can monkeys climb that tall tree

7. How many tigers are in the cage

8. Have you seen the dolphin show

9. Which animal did you like best

10. Elephants are gigantic animals

11. That chimpanzee makes me laugh

12. What time is it

13. We have to be home by 6:00

14. Can you come again next Saturday

Draw your favorite zoo animal on the back of this page.

©1995 by Evan-Moor Corp.   Language Fundamentals

Dot-to-Dot Fun

Start at a.
Connect the dots.

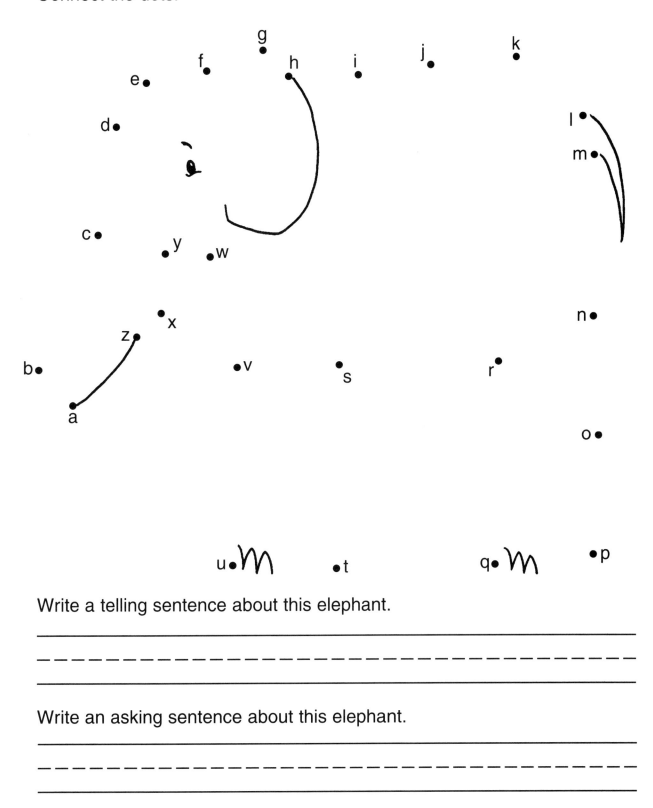

Write a telling sentence about this elephant.

_____

_ _

_____

Write an asking sentence about this elephant.

_____

_ _

_____

©1995 by Evan-Moor Corp.   Language Fundamentals

Exclamation Marks

We use an **exclamation point** to show strong feeling.
Put an exclamation point at the end of each phrase and sentence.

Stop that

How beautiful you are

Look out

Let me go

Don't touch it

Oh, no

Put it down

Be careful

I hate snakes

Wow

That was scary

Ouch, that hurt

Write a sentence that needs an exclamation point.

_____

_____

_____

_____

Using an Exclamation Point

This is an exclamation point: !
An exclamation shows strong feeling.

Put an ! at the end of each of these exclamations.

1. Stop that cat !

2. This house is a mess

3. We need help

4. I hate pickles

5. Be careful

6. Don't shout

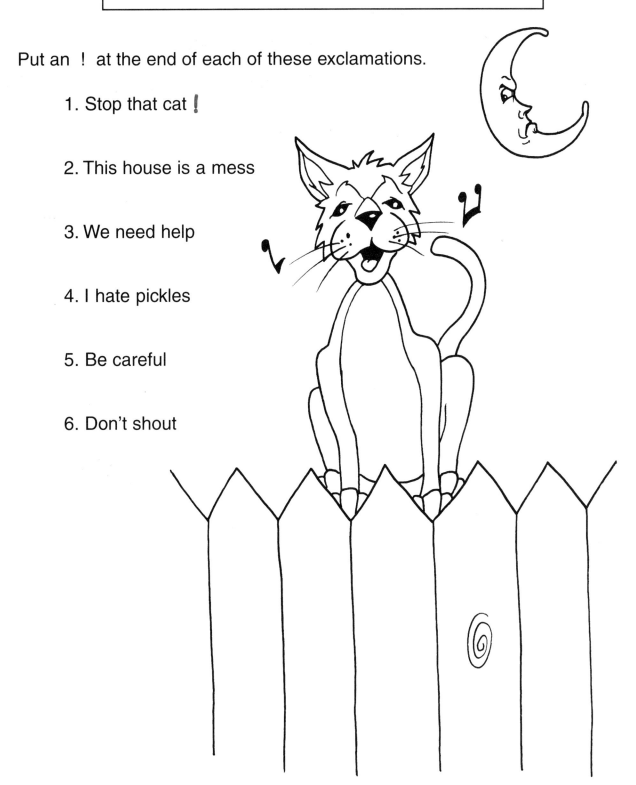

Correct the Sentence

Write capital letters.
Use periods or question marks.

the fox is in a box

can it get out

is that a cat

no, it is a skunk

do you like to jump rope

i think it is fun

when did you get that toy

can I play with it

©1995 by Evan-Moor Corp. Language Fundamentals

Punctuation

> Every sentence ends with a punctuation mark.
> **period** - Pizza tastes good.
> **question mark** - Do you like pizza?
> **exclamation point** - This pizza is too hot!

Put the correct punctuation mark at the end of each sentence.

1. Did you bring your lunch today ?

2. All of the library books were due today

3. Put that down right now

4. Haven't you finished your homework yet

5. Look who's here

6. Did you have fun at the party

7. That movie was really scary

8. Where do you live

©1995 by Evan-Moor Corp.

Language Fundamentals

Write Your Own Sentences

Write sentences about this picture.
Use the correct end punctuation and capital letters.

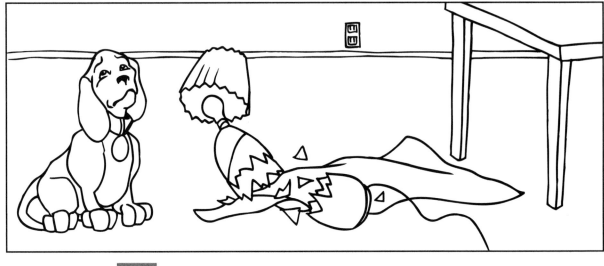

a question ?

_____

- -

_____

- -

_____

a statement .

_____

- -

_____

- -

_____

an exclamation !

_____

- -

_____

- -

_____

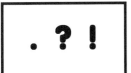

What Did You Say?

Put in the punctuation for each sentence.

What is your favorite day of the week

I like Saturday best
My friend Tony and I go to the beach
We climb on the rocks and make sand castles

Are you a good climber

We like to look in the tide pools
We find interesting plants

Have you ever seen a live crab

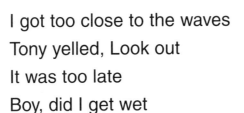

Tony found one last week
Did you know crabs can pinch
Tony dropped that crab very fast

I got too close to the waves
Tony yelled, Look out
It was too late
Boy, did I get wet

Do you want to go with us next time
Will you mom let you come
We will let you pick up any crabs we find
We will have a great time

Draw a crab with pinchers on the back of this page.

©1995 by Evan-Moor Corp.
Language Fundamentals

Summer Fun

Read each sentence and add the punctuation.

Do you like summer ?

It is my favorite time of year

Can you guess why

I love picnics

All my friends like picnics too

Have you ever gone on a picnic

What food did you take

Did you drop scraps on the ground

We find such good food when people leave

Draw a picnic lunch on the tablecloth.

©1995 by Evan-Moor Corp. Language Fundamentals

Winter Fun

Add the punctuation.

Look

It is snowing

Winter is here at last

It is cold outside in the snow

Do you have mittens to keep your fingers warm

I have red wool mittens

What kind do you have

Do you have boots and a hat too

Can you come to my house to play

Bring your sled

We can slide down the hill by the school

We can make a snow monster later

Will your mom let you come

Come on, Mike

Let's go ask her now

Draw a snow monster on the back of this page.

Correct These Sentences

Read these out loud to hear if there is more than one sentence in the line.
Put a capital at the beginning of each sentence.
Put a punctuation mark at the end of each sentence.
Capitalize other words that need capitals.

1. where did you get that book can I read it

2. i must be at school by 8:30 what time is it now

3. john has a sandwich for lunch what do you have

4. don't climb up that old ladder it isn't safe

5. i like the present you made for me

6. when are you going to the party can i come too

7. my dentist gave me a new toothbrush

8. raul fell off his bike he broke his arm

The Dream

. ? !

Read this story out loud to help you know when one sentence ends and a new one begins. Put a capital at the beginning of each sentence. Put a punctuation mark at the end of each sentence.

what a strange place this is it doesn't look like Earth why

is it so dark what is that furry shape over there by the rocks it's

moving closer help i can't get away why won't my feet move I'm

caught in sticky mud can anyone hear me hurry save me

what a scary dream i am glad i woke up I'm never going to

eat a peanut butter and pickle sandwich again

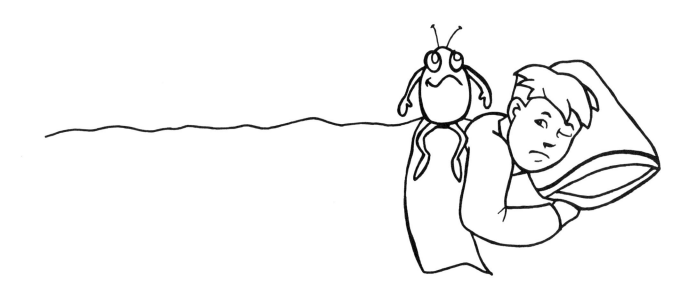

©1995 by Evan-Moor Corp.   Language Fundamentals

Commands

A command tells someone to do something. It ends in a period.

Circle the sentences that give a command.

1. Give me that book.

2. That cake looks delicious.

3. Bring me my new shoes.

4. My bicycle is red and black.

5. How do you get to the mall from here?

6. Put your toys away.

7. This is too hot.

8. Get out of the street.

9. Stay away from that broken glass.

10. Don't put your feet on the coffee table.

11. What are you going to do this afternoon?

12. Do your homework before you go out to play.

Name the Sentence

A **statement** tells something. It ends in a period.

A **question** asks something. It ends in a question mark.

A **command** tells someone to do something. It ends in a period.

An **exclamation** shows strong feeling. It ends in an exclamation point.

Put the correct punctuation at the end of each sentence.
Tell which type of sentence it is.

1. What time does the movie start _____

2. Let's meet at Jamal's house _____

3. Don't put your feet on the furniture _____

4. This is hard work _____

5. Wow, what a great present _____

6. Maria and Ana went to Mexico for Easter _____

7. Can you explain how to do this problem _____

8. Put those books on the shelf _____

The Job

Write sentences about this picture.

a question ❓

_____
_____
_____
_____

a statement or command ▪

_____
_____
_____
_____

an exclamation ❗

_____
_____
_____
_____

Commas

Use commas between the name of a city and state or a province.

Dallas, Texas

Put commas where they belong:

1. Columbus Ohio

2. Honolulu Hawaii

3. Calgary Alberta

4. Springfield Illinois

5. Salt Lake City Utah

6. Toronto Ontario

Write where you live:

_____

_ _

_____

Use commas between the day and the year.

May 5, 1996

Put commas in these dates:

1. April 1 1993

2. June 16 1940

3. February 11 1994

4. July 4 1776

5. March 31 1874

6. December 25 2000

Write your birthdate here:

_____

_ _

_____

©1995 by Evan-Moor Corp.   Language Fundamentals

Commas in a Series

Use commas between three or more items that come in a series.

shirt, hat, and pants

Put commas in these sentences:

1. I went to the zoo with Margo, Alex, and Ernie.

2. George planted peas carrots and corn in his garden.

3. We ate hot dogs peanuts and pretzels at the ball game.

4. Birds can fly sing and build nests.

5. Mrs. Gomez has roses daisies and carnations in her front yard.

6. Carla Sean Tina and Harry helped clean up the beach on Saturday.

7. Have you had the measles mumps or chicken pox?

8. Moose elk and deer all have antlers.

Using Commas in Sentences

Put commas in the right places as you write these sentences.

1. Write a sentence about your favorite foods using at least three things in a series.

_____

- -

_____

- -

_____

- -

_____

2. Write a sentence about your friends using at leasts three names in a series.

_____

- -

_____

- -

_____

- -

_____

3. Write a sentence about animals putting at least three things in a series.

_____

- -

_____

- -

_____

- -

_____

Quotation Marks

Use quotation marks at the beginning
and at the end of a person's exact words.

Maria said, "Can you come to my house after school?"
Tony answered, "I'll have to ask my mother."

Write each sentence.
Put each person's exact words in quotation marks.

1. Lee said, I'll get us something to drink.

   Lee said, "I'll get us something to drink."

2. Do you have a pet dog? asked Margaret.

3. Shawna shouted, Keep away from that broken glass!

4. Why do I have to go to bed so early? complained Susan.

5. Willie said, I like to play soccer with my friends.

6. Michael asked, How soon will it be lunch time?

Answer Key
Part One

Page 5

Bob and Amy are my pet kittens.

My funny, little puppy likes to play with his rubber bone.

On Sunday morning, Mr. Brown cooks breakfast for his wife.

All the circus elephants marched down the street.

The students in Room 5 are going on a class trip.

Page 6

2., 3., 5., 7., 8. ⑤

Page 7

3., 5., 6., 9., 10., 12., 13., 15. ⑧

Page 8

1., 5., 6., 9., 13., 14., 15. ⑦

Page 9

2., 4., 6., 7., 9., 10. 11., 13., 14., 15.

Page 10

Sam and George were best friends

The school bus had a flat tire.

A trail of ants crawled into the picnic basket.

Invaders from space flew over my house.

The band of gorillas looked for fruit to eat.

A helicopter landed in the park last night.

Page 20

1. My pet is not big.

2 It cannot run and hop.

3. My pet can swim.

4. It is as yellow as butter.

5. Can you tell what my pet is?

DOT-to-DOT = a fish

Page 21

1. The girl was sad when her friend moved away.

2. A cow with black and white spots was eating grass.

3. Johnny and Mary went to the park to play.

4. Saturday was so hot we all went to the beach.

5. Does it ever rain in the desert?

6. Can you help me with my homework?

7. Betty has a new pet snake.

8. How fast can you run around the track?

Page 26

1. My name is Harry Hopper.

2. Can you go to the movies Saturday night?

3. Marta lives on Washington Street

4. I am going to Canada on my vacation.

5. Does your uncle live in Vermont?

6. Marshall's birthday is on Monday.

7. Did Mary Jo and Ben move to Toronto?

Page 27

1. My cousin, Pedro, lives in San Diego, California.

2. Teresa said, "I am going to Texas in July."

3. Mrs. Brown was born in Florida, but now she lives in Canada.

4. Can you come to my house for Easter dinner?

Page 28

1. My teacher, Professor Green, Lives in Dallas, Texas.

2. Kisha and Tamara went to Disneyland for a vacation.

3. Mr. Martin cooked Thanksgiving dinner.

4. School will be out at the end of May.

Page 35

1. Can you play jump rope?

2. I like to run and hop.

3. Morris has a pet frog.

4. What is in the box?

5. Alma has a baby sister.

6. Where did it go?

Page 36

period - 2, 4, 5, 10, 11, 13

question mark - 1, 3, 6, 7, 8, 9, 12, 14

Page 40

The fox is in a box.

Can it get out?

Is that a cat?

No, it is a skunk.

Do you like to jump rope?

I think it is fun.

When did you get that toy?

Can I play with it?

Page 41

period - 2
question mark - 1, 4, 6, 8
exclamation mark - 3, 5, 7

Page 43

What is your favorite day of the week?
I like Saturday best.
My friend Tony and I go to the beach.
We climb on the rocks and make sand castles.
Are you a good climber?
We like to look in the tide pools.
We find interesting plants.
Have you ever seen a live crab?
Tony found one last week.
Did you know crabs can pinch?
Tony dropped that crab very fast.
I got too close to the waves.
Tony yelled, "Look out"!
It was too late.
Boy, did I get wet!
Do you want to go with us next time?
Will you mom let you come?
We will let you pick up any crabs we find.
We will have a great time!

Page 44

Do you like summer?
It is my favorite time of year.
Can you guess why?
I love picnics!
All my friends like picnics too.
Have you ever gone on a picnic?
What food did you take?
Did you drop scraps on the ground?
We find such good food when people leave.

Page 46

Look!
It is snowing!
Winter is here at last!
It is cold outside in the snow.
Do you have mittens to keep your fingers warm?
I have red wool mittens.
What kind do you have?
Do you have boots and a hat too?
Can you come to my house to play?
Bring your sled.
We can slide down the hill by the school.
We can make a snow monster later.
Will you mom let you come?
Come on, Mike.
Let's go ask her now.

Page 47

1. Where did you get that book? Can I read it?
2. I must be at school by 8:30. What time is it now?
3. John has a sandwich for lunch. What do you have?
4. Don't climb up that old ladder! It isn't safe.
5. I like the present you made for me.
6. When are you going to the party? Can I come too?
7. My dentist gave me a new toothbrush.
8. Raul fell off his bike. He broke his arm.

Page 48

What a strange place this is. It doesn't look like Earth. Why is it so dark? What is that furry shape over by the rocks? It's moving closer! Help! I can't get away! Why won't my feet move? I'm caught in sticky mud! Can anyone hear me? Hurry! Save me! What a scary dream! I am glad I woke up! I'm never going to eat a peanut butter and pickle sandwich again!

Page 49

1, 3, 6, 8, 9, 10, 12

Page 50

1. question   5. exclamation
2. statement   6. statement
3. command   7. question
4. exclamation   8. command

Page 53

1. I went to the zoo with Margo, Alex, and Ernie.
2. George planted peas, carrots, and corn in his garden.
3. We ate hot dogs, peanuts, and pretzels at the ball game.
4. Birds can fly, sing, and build nests.
5. Mrs. Gomez has roses, daisies, and carnations in her front yard.
6. Carla, Sean, Tina, and Harry helped clean up the beach on Saturday.
7. Have you had the measles, mumps, or chicken pox?
8. Moose, elk and deer all have antlers.

Page 55

1. Lee said, "I'll get us something to drink."
2. "Do you have a pet dog?" asked Margaret.
3. Shawna shouted, "Keep away from that broken glass!"
4. "Why do I have to go to bed so early?" complained Susan.
5. Willie said, "I like to play soccer with my friends."
6. Michael asked, "How soon will it be lunch time?"

The **Answer Key** for this section is found on pages 129-132.

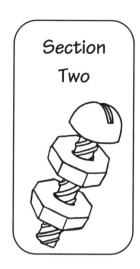

Grammar

What do we mean by "grammar"?
Grammar is the study of the forms and uses of words in sentences. It is knowing rules about the use of words and using words according to these rules.

What is included in this section?
This section contains the different parts of speech. Activities are provided to practice recognizing and using them.

- Nouns and Pronouns

- Verbs

- Adjectives

- Adverbs (at an introductory level)

- Subject and Predicate

Using the pages in this section:
When selecting pages to use with your students, consider which areas they need to practice and at what level that practice needs to be. The variety of pages available for use allows you to individualize practice activities to better meet your students' needs.

At the simplest level there are pages asking children to identify naming words and action words.

At the highest level there are pages requiring students to identify and use: common and proper nouns; past and present tenses of verbs; both adjectives and adverbs to describe; subjects and predicates of sentences.

Group and Center Activities

The activities listed below can be used with any part of speech by changing the set of pictures or words on the cards. You will find cards on the following pages:

- *Pages 59-91*   **Nouns and Pronouns**
- *Pages 92-107*   **Verbs**
- *Pages 108-128*   **Adjectives and Adverbs**

"Describe Me"
Select a student to come up in front of the group. Ask the rest of the group to...

       name the person *(noun)*
       describe the person *(adjective)*
       tell something the person can do *(verb)*

Repeat this activity with each person (or several people) in the group.

"Sort the Cards"
Put words on cards or sentence strips (or use the cards listed above). Have children read the words and determine which ones fit the stated criteria. For example...

nouns and verbs - Have students read the words and decide if the word is a naming word (noun) or an action word (verb).
nouns and pronouns - Have students read the words and divide the cards into two sets, one containing nouns, the other containing pronouns.
adjectives - Have students read the words and separate the cards into sets by the characteristic being described (color, size, quantity, etc.).

"Read and Draw"
1. Put all of the noun cards in a bag. Each child pulls out a card, reads the noun, and draws its picture.
2. Put out a bag of nouns and a bag of adjectives. Each child pulls one card from each bag, reads the cards, and illustrates what they say.
3. Put out a bag of nouns, one of adjectives and one of verbs. Each child picks a word from each bag, reads the cards, and makes an appropriate illustration.

"What Do You See?"
Show a picture to the class. Have them name items in the picture according to the part of speech you are practicing. List these on a chart or the chalkboard. For example, you might have them give you the names of all the items and people in the picture. Or you might ask them to tell you every action they see. Or have students describe objects or actions in the picture.

Nouns and Pronouns

Nouns are words used to name a person, place, thing, quality, or event.
- common and proper nouns
- singular and plural nouns
- nouns showing ownership

A pronoun is a word used instead of a noun (*he, she, they, it*).

"Brainstorm"

Create class lists of nouns. Write these words on charts according to the type of noun (people, place, things, animals, proper nouns, etc.). Select "artists" to illustrate the nouns and paste these pictures next to the words on the charts. Display the charts to use with "Reading the Room" and as a reference for your young authors.

"More Than One"

You can use this same process for making plural forms from any nouns (add *s*, *es*, change *y* to *i* and add *es*, etc.)

Call up one boy. Ask "What is this?" Write **boy** on the chalkboard. Call up another boy. Ask "What are these?" Ask students how you can change the word **boy** to **boys**. Select a child to come up and add the **s** with colored chalk. Repeat the process using objects around the room (or use pictures of objects) that are made plural by adding **s**.

Use any or all of the cards on pages 65-68 for matching practice of singular and plural forms.

"Meese? Mice? Mouses?"

Write the word **mouses** on the board. Ask students to tell you if this is the correct way to write "more than one mouse." When someone gives you the correct form - **mice** - write it on the board. Continue through each of the words represented on the plural cards (pages 65 and 67).

Note: Reproduce these **noun picture cards**.

©1995 by Evan-Moor Corp. Language Fundamentals

Note: Reproduce these **noun picture cards**.

©1995 by Evan-Moor Corp.

Language Fundamentals

chair	rabbit
mouse	skate
clown	tree
bus	candy
hat	bird

girl	doctor
house	book
fruit	gorilla
pony	purse
grapes	dog

he	she
me	I
it	we
us	they
them	you

Note: Reproduce these **picture cards** to use with group and center activities.

©1995 by Evan-Moor Corp.

Language Fundamentals

Note: Reproduce these **picture cards** to use in group and center activities

teeth	geese	children
tooth	goose	child
mice	men	women
mouse	man	woman

pony	bunny	berry
ponies	bunnies	berries
baby	fly	cherry
babies	flies	cherries

What's My Name?

A word that names something is called a **noun**.

Write the noun that names these pictures.

Naming Words

People are <u>who</u>.	Things are <u>what</u>.

who (put circle around)	**what** (put X on)
(Bob)	you and me
~~red top~~	train
big box	yellow car
clown	Doctor Brown
girl	trees
bike	boy and girl
Dad	books

Person, Place, or Thing

A noun names a person, place, or thing.

Match:

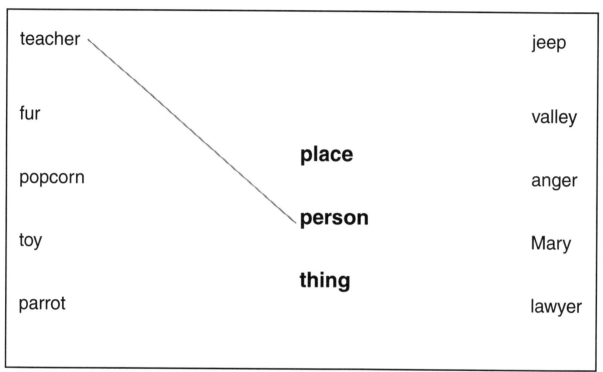

teacher		jeep
fur		valley
	place	
popcorn		anger
	person	
toy		Mary
	thing	
parrot		lawyer

I am a person.

That is a place.

This is a thing.

©1995 by Evan-Moor Corp.
Language Fundamentals

Nouns

A noun is a word that names a person, place, or thing.

place

person

thing

Circle the nouns in these sentences.

1. The (girl) ate an (apple,) a (banana,) and a (sandwich).

2. Give the book to that man next to the white building.

3. Have you ever been to the park in Boston?

4. My train was late one day this week because of snow.

5. My pet cat has three kittens in the garage.

6. The helicopter landed in a field near my house.

©1995 by Evan-Moor Corp. Language Fundamentals

One and More Than One

Some nouns name one person, place, or thing.
boy   chair   book

Some nouns name more than one person, place, or thing.
boys   chairs   books

Read these nouns that name one thing.
Add an **s** to a word to make it name **more than one**.

tree   _trees_

river   _____

flower   _____

boat   _____

pet   _____

street   _____

rose   _____

cake   _____

More Than One

Add **s** to make more than one.

2 _ _ _ _ _ _ _ _ _

3 _ _ _ _ _ _ _ _ _

2 _ _ _ _ _ _ _ _ _

3 _ _ _ _ _ _ _ _ _

2 _ _ _ _ _ _ _ _ _

2 _ _ _ _ _ _ _ _ _

©1995 by Evan-Moor Corp.

Language Fundamentals

More Than One

Add **es** to make more than one when a noun ends with **sh**, **ch**, **x**, **s**, or **ss**.

box

dish

fox

bus

watch

bench

Special Words for More Than One

Cut out the words.
Paste them under the pictures.

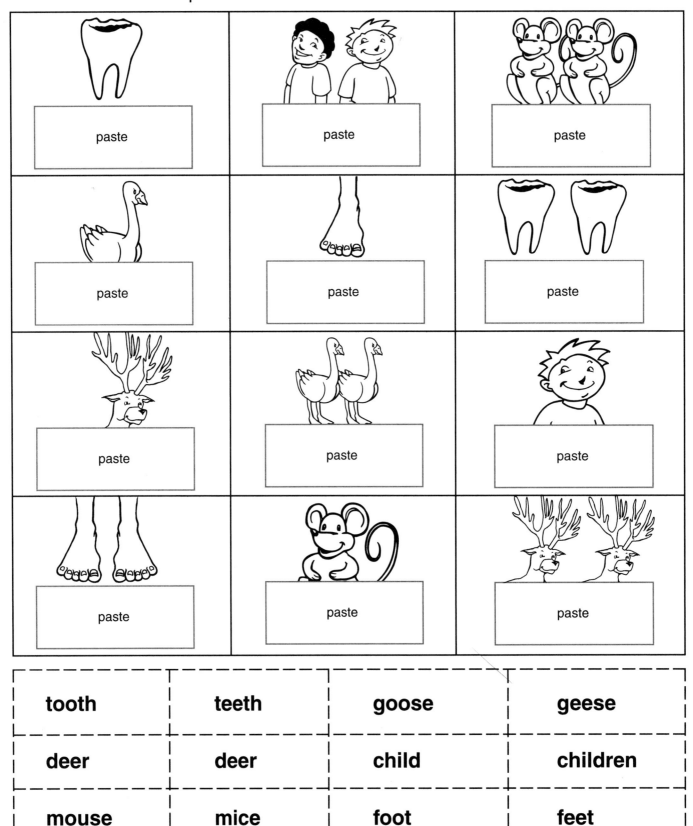

tooth	teeth	goose	geese
deer	deer	child	children
mouse	mice	foot	feet

©1995 by Evan-Moor Corp. 76 Language Fundamentals

Fill in the Blank.

Use the correct word in each sentence.

tooth	geese	child	women
teeth	foot	children	mouse
goose	feet	woman	mice

1. I brush my _____ every day.

   I lost a _____ yesterday.

2. Mrs. Martinez called the _____ in from recess.

   One _____ missed the party.

3. Ali has a pet _____ in a cage.

   There were a lot of field _____ in the barn.

4. How many _____ are in the pen?

   We read a story about a _____ that laid golden eggs.

5. The _____ at the pet store sold me a goldfish.

   The _____ were working together to make cookies for the bake sale.

Words that End with Y

These nouns end with **y**.
This is how to make them name "more than one."

1. Drop the **y**.
2. Add **ies**.

city   cities

fairy

pony

cherry

baby

fly

berry

bunny

Plural Nouns

Add **s**, **es**, or **ies** to these nouns to complete the sentences.

fox

1. Two **foxes** ran across our backyard.

cherry

2. We went to Mr. Lee's orchard to pick _____.

bus

3. It took six _____ to take our school to the play.

toy

4. We repaired old _____ and sold them at the

   yard sale.

bush

5. I earned five dollars trimming _____ for

   my neighbor.

puppy

6. His dog had four _____.

story

7. The librarian reads _____ to the little

   children every afternoon.

guess

8. You get three _____ to answer the riddle.

Who Owns It?

We show that someone owns something by adding **'s** to their name.

Add **'s** to show who owns these things.

1. ___Bob's___ bike
   Bob

2. _____ carrot
   Bunny

3. _____ doll
   girl

4. _____ lunch
   Father

5. _____ jacket
   Ann

6. _____ tractor
   farmer

7. _____ purse
   Mother

8. _____ house
   dog

©1995 by Evan-Moor Corp. Language Fundamentals

Ownership

When a noun names more than one and ends in an **s**,
put the apostrophe after the **s**.

singular - 's	dog**'s**	Tom**'s**	man**'s**
plural - s'	boy**s'**	babie**s'**	parent**s'**

Add the apostrophes:

boys	1. two _____ coats
pets	2. my _____ collar
babys	3. the _____ bottle
bunnies	4. the _____ carrots
parents	5. my _____ car
birds	6. that _____ cage
artists	7. those _____ paints
boys	8. a _____ bike

Proper Nouns

Proper nouns name special people, places, or things.
Proper nouns always begin with a capital letter.

Mrs. **F**einstein   **O**klahoma   **M**ississippi River

Circle the proper nouns in these sentences.

1. What color is your (Uncle Ned's) house?

2. Jamal and Tanisha live on Wilson Street.

3. Lake Louise is in British Columbia.

4. Mr. Garcia went for a visit to Tijuana, Mexico.

5. I went to see Dr. Brown to get my teeth cleaned.

6. Did you invite Paul and Angela to your party?

7. Mom and Dad are going to San Francisco next Sunday.

8. Lee named his new dogs Stan and Ollie.

Proper Nouns

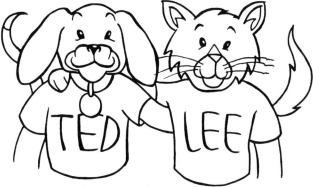

Write a proper noun for each noun below.
Don't forget the capital letters.

boys   Ted and Lee

a river

a school

a doctor

a city

a book title

a country

a television show

©1995 by Evan-Moor Corp.   Language Fundamentals

Different Kinds of Nouns

Common Noun - names a person, place, or thing.

table   boy   cat

Proper Noun - names a special person, place, or thing. Proper nouns start with capital letters.

Mary   **T**exas   **S**unday

Underline all the nouns in these sentences.
Now circle the proper nouns you underlined.

1. (Marcos) played soccer on (Saturday.)

2. Sally went to Texas to see her grandfather.

3. The Mississippi River goes through many states.

4. Tony read a book called *Hiawatha*.

5. A duck was swimming on Miller's Pond.

6. The children were going to Kyle's party.

7. Squirrels live in the trees down the middle of Elm Boulevard.

8. Mark and his father are going to wash the car.

©1995 by Evan-Moor Corp.   Language Fundamentals

Who is it?

Match.

he

she

we

it

Write.   **he   she   we   it**

1.  _____ _ _ _ _ _ _ _____	2.  _____ _ _ _ _ _ _ _____
3. 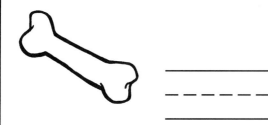 _____ _ _ _ _ _ _ _____	4.  _____ _ _ _ _ _ _ _____

Pronouns

Pronouns are words that take the place of nouns.

He   **She**   **We**   **it**

Write a pronoun on each line.

1. Mom has a basket.

____She____ puts food in____it____.

2. Kim had a green ball.

_____plays with _____.

3. Bob and I got a pizza.

_____ ate all of_____.

We Love it!

4. Carlos has a rabbit.

_____ feeds _____ carrots.

©1995 by Evan-Moor Corp.   Language Fundamentals

Pronouns

Read the sentence pairs below.
Underline the nouns and draw a circle around the pronouns.

1. The sun was very hot.

   It was very hot.

2. Sam and Ollie like to play outside.

   They like to play outside.

3. Pete and I want to go swimming.

   We want to go swimming.

4. Mr. Green went to the park.

   He went to the park.

5. Ann is going to school.

   She is going to school.

Pronouns

Write the pronoun that takes the place of the underlined noun.

1. <u>Mary</u> can ride a bike.

2. <u>Lunch</u> was very good today.

3. The <u>fish</u> in my aquarium are hungry.

4. <u>Father</u> works at the post office.

5. <u>Lee and I</u> are on the same soccer team.

6. <u>Andy</u> wants to go to Disneyland for his birthday.

I	you	he	she	it	we	they

©1995 by Evan-Moor Corp.   88   Language Fundamentals

Possessive Pronouns Show Ownership

my	your	her	his	its	our	their

Write a pronoun in each sentence below.

1. Tom rode _____**his**_____ bike around the block.

   his   **its**

2. Sam and Terry can't find _____ jackets.

   its   **their**

3. "When is _____birthday?" Tom asked the little girl.

   her   **your**

4. _____ friends are coming to the park with us.

   Its   **Our**

5. When will _____ haircut be finished?

   her   **their**

6. A bird ate _____ worm.

   his   **its**

Happy Birthday

More Pronouns

me	you	him	her	it	us	them

You want <u>it</u>!

Write the pronoun for these words.

_____them_____ 1. the boxes

_____ 2. mother and father

_____ 3. Kisha

_____ 4. Thomas

_____ 5. the bike

_____ 6. Bob and me

_____ 7. Uncle Sam

_____ 8. Sally

_____ 9. the tall trees

_____ 10. you and me

_____ 11. the dog and cat

_____ 12. the present

©1995 by Evan-Moor Corp.   Language Fundamentals

Using I and Me

Use **I** as the subject of a sentence.
Use **me** as part of the predicate.

Write **I** or **me** in the sentences below.

1. _____ like to play games

2. Amy wants _____ to come to her party.

3. _____ have to go home now.

4. Will you help _____ with my homework?

Name yourself last when you are talking
about another person and yourself.

Pete and I got a new dog.
Dad gave it to Pete and me.

1. Anna gave my sister and _____ her old bike.

2. Mother picked up Sam and _____ after school.

3. Saturday afternoon my sister and _____ mowed the lawn.

4. The package was for Carlos and _____.

Verbs

- words used to express action or being
- forms of "to be"
- past and present tense

run
jump
fly

"Let's Move"

Explain that some words name the things we do, our "actions." These words have a special name. They are called "verbs." Have volunteers come to the front of the group, one at a time, and show an action they can do. Have the rest of the class copy these actions. Write the name of each action on a chart titled "Actions" or "Verbs." Add to the chart throughout the year.

"What Am I Doing?"

Put the verb cards (pages 93-94) in a box. Have a child draw out one of the cards, read it, and act out the motion. Have the rest of the group try to guess what the card said.

"More Verb Card Games"

Use the verb cards for these activities from page 58:
    Read and Draw
    Sort the Cards

"Action Detectives"

Have children observe their classmates and the adults at school, both in class and outside the classroom, to see what kinds of actions are being done. Come together after the observation period and add any new actions they observed to your action chart.

"There's More Than One Way to Say That"

Put any overworked verb on the chalkboard. Have your students think about other words that mean the same thing, have similar meanings, or would add interest to spoken or written language. Make a list of these words and post them in the classroom for reference when students are writing.

ran	*said*
hurried	answered
galloped	shouted

talk	sing
fix	wash
hurry	eat
plant	dance
work	visit

play	brush
go	catch
rest	see
work	want
came	clean

What Are You Doing?

Words that tell what you are doing are called **verbs**.

Put a circle around the <u>doing</u> words.

swim	**green**	**sing**
sleep	**jump**	**chair**
speak	**coat**	**wink**

Draw.

dance	**ride**

What Can You Do?

Make a list of ten things you can do.

1. _____

2. _____

3. _____

4. _____

5. _____

6. _____

7. _____

8. _____

9. _____

_____

Make a picture.

I am _____.

Using Is and Are

one - **is**   more than one - **are**

Circle the right word.

1. The pet cat ((is) are) small.

2. Ann and Jill (is are) here.

3. My bike (is   are) red.

4. The dogs (is   are) running.

5. We (is   are) going to sleep.

6. Mom and Dad (is   are) at work.

©1995 by Evan-Moor Corp.   Language Fundamentals

Using Was and Were

one - **was**   more than one - **were**

The monkey **was** in the tree.

The monkeys **were** in the tree.

Circle the right word.

1. Her bike (was   were) big.

2. Carlos and Maria (was   were) playing.

3. We (was   were) at the park.

4. The cake (was   were) yummy.

5. I (was   were) at home.

6. My pet cats (was   were) funny.

©1995 by Evan-Moor Corp. Language Fundamentals

Which Verb?

one person - **s**   more than one person - no **s**

Sally **sits** in a chair.

Betty and Sally **sit** in a chair.

Write the word.

1. **run - runs**

    Tom _____ fast.

    Kim and Ann _____ too.

2. **hop - hops**

    Kangaroos _____ up and down.

    A frog _____ too.

3. **ride - rides**

    Lee _____ her bike.

    Her friends _____ bikes too.

4. **nap - naps**

    My kittens _____ every day.

    My baby sister _____ too.

Verb Endings

Today I am play**ing**.
Yesterday I play**ed**.

Add **ed** and **ing**

1. jumping - jumped

The girl is _jumping_ rope.

Sandy_____ rope.

2. hopping - hopped

The frog_____.

The frog is _____.

3. looking - looked

Pat is_____ for her cat.

She has _____ all day.

4. playing - played

I _____with my kite.

I am _____with a top.

©1995 by Evan-Moor Corp. Language Fundamentals

More Verb Endings

Add **es** to verbs that end in **s**, **sh**, **ch**, or **x**.

catch - catch**es**   fix - fix**es**
wash - wash**es**   toss - toss**es**

When the verb ends in **y**, take away the **y** and add **ies**.
cry - cr**ies**   carry - carr**ies**

Add **es** or **ies** to these verbs.

1. fix   fixes

2. hurry

3. try

4. reach

5. dry

6. rush

7. fry

8. wash

9. mix

10. pass

11. box

12. marry

Helping Verbs

Has, **had**, and **have** are helping verbs.
Use them with verbs such as:

     run   come   seen   gone

You don't need a helping word with these verbs.

     ran   came   saw   went

Circle the correct verb.

1. Ann (come (came)) to my house.

2. The horse (run ran) across the field.

3. Jamal has (gone went) to see a movie.

4. We (seen saw) a rainbow in the sky.

5. Sally has (seen saw) my new kittens.

6. Mr. and Mrs. Smith have (come came) to have dinner.

7. They (went gone) to fish at the lake.

8. I like to (run ran) as fast as I can.

Have you seen the cheese?

Match the Verbs

Present - is happening now

Past - already happened

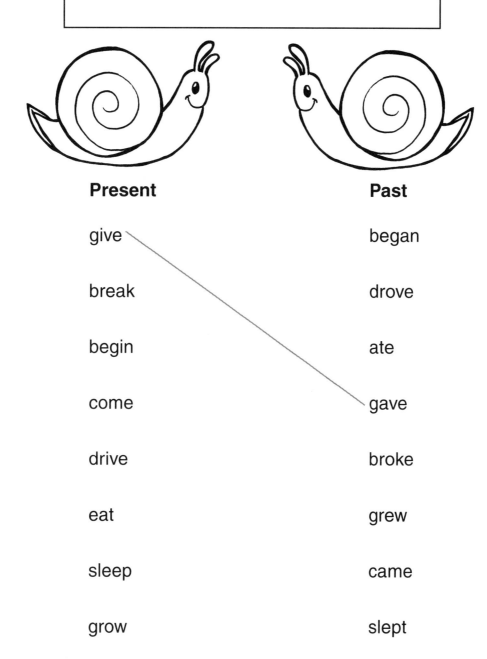

Present	Past
give	began
break	drove
begin	ate
come	gave
drive	broke
eat	grew
sleep	came
grow	slept

©1995 by Evan-Moor Corp.

Language Fundamentals

Helping Verbs

have	has	had

These verbs help the main verb tell what someone or something does.

I **have** always loved bow ties.

Underline the helping verbs in these sentences.

1. Mrs. Brown had baked a pie for dinner.

2. I have read a story every day this week.

3. She has taken the books back to the library.

4. The artists have finished their paintings.

5. Pete had to go to the dentist.

6. Who has been to Texas?

7. Pam and Kim have been friends a long time.

8. Have you been to the new store in the mall?

©1995 by Evan-Moor Corp. Language Fundamentals

It Happened in the Past

Add **ed** to a verb to show that something happened in the past.

I walk to school.   Yesterday I walked to school.

Fill in the blanks:

1. My mother and father _____looked_____ at the puppy.
   look   looked

2. I _____ for my friend yesterday.
   wait   waited

3. She _____at home.
   stay   stayed

4. Pat and Bill _____to the store this morning.
   walk   walked

5. He _____ over the fence.
   jump jumped

6. They _____ at the joke.
   laugh   laughed

7. They _____ the dessert at dinner last night.
   like   liked

The Verb "To Be"

The verb "to be" joins the subject of the sentence with the words that describe it. The verb "to be" has many forms.

be   **am**   **is**

I am.   I will be.   He is.

Underline the **to be** verbs in the sentences below.

1. All my friends are helpful.

2. The Bayview School team was the best.

3. The pizza and sodas were tasty.

4. Were you at the swimming pool on Saturday?

5. I am happy when Grandmother comes to see me.

6. Pam is singing and dancing.

The Verb "To Be"

The toys **are** in the wagon.

Write the **to be** verbs in the blanks.

1. The boys and girls _____ ready for the game.
   was   were

2. We_____ going to the library.
   is   are

3. It _____ fun to swim in the lake.
   is   are

4. Who _____ first in line?
   was   were

5. I _____ singing in the play.
   am   are

6. Please_____ ready on time.
   be   were

7. It_____ very hot yesterday.
   was   were

8. Some hens _____ laying eggs.
   was   were

Adjectives and Adverbs

- **Adjectives**
  words used to describe a person, animal, or thing
    by size, shape, color, quantity, etc.
  using *a, an, the*

- **Adverbs**
  words telling how, when, or where something happens
  words telling how much or how little is meant

"Who Am I?"
Describe a child in the classroom by physical characteristics and personal traits. Have your students try to guess who you are describing. After you have modeled this activity, call up students to do the describing.

"What Am I?"
Place several objects (or pictures of objects) where the group can see them. Describe one of the objects and have students guess what it is. Begin with objects with gross differences and progress to those having minor differences.

"Adjective Cards"
Use the adjective cards (pages 109-110) for these activities from page 58:

- Sort the Cards
- Read and Draw

I am a tall, handsome, strong, young man.
I can run quickly.

hot	big
white	six
soft	hard
pretty	bumpy
cold	fast

tall	red
busy	angry
fluffy	smooth
fresh	wet
ripe	dirty

What Does It Look Like?

Circle the picture that matches the words.

It is big.

It is tall.

It is black.

It is hot.

It is soft.

I see three.

Follow the Dots

Start at 1.
Connect the dots.
Color the picture.
Finish the sentences.

QUACK!

3
2
9
1
4
30
8
10
29
5
28
7
6
27
11
26
12
13 18 24 25
19 23 22
14
17 20
21
15
16

I see a _____ duck.

It can _____ .

©1995 by Evan-Moor Corp.

Language Fundamentals

Words that Describe

Match the pictures and words.
Put a line under the word that tells how something looks.

six bugs

a brown hen

a cold snack

a big box

a happy smile

Find the Adjectives

Circle the words that tell how something looks.

fat	duck	box	funny
hot	fast	sleepy	yellow
big	rock	run	long
soft	dog	six	busy
tall	red	old	ten

Draw.

a small cat on a soft blue rug

Adjectives

An adjective describes a noun.
It tells <u>how many</u> or <u>what kind</u>.

He took **three white** ducks to the **summer** fair.

Draw a circle around the adjectives in the sentences below.

1. The busy street was filled with fast cars.

2. The tired woman sat on the wooden bench to rest.

3. Kelly ate a big yellow banana and drank some cool milk.

4. Jay was the only boy in the band from a small school.

5. The happy girl won a shiny new bike in the big contest.

6. Lee's frisky puppy raced across the green grass.

Adjectives

The words **a**, **an**, and **the** are adjectives too.
They are also called **articles**.

a   an   the

Write **a**, **an**, or **the** on the blanks in these sentences.

1. I wear __a__ raincoat and take _____ umbrella with me when it rains.

2. Did _____ sun shine every day in July?

3. I had _____ apple and _____ sandwich for lunch.

4. Don't forget to take _____ gift to _____ birthday party.

5. Carlos gets _____ allowance every Saturday.

6. _____ grass needs to be mowed.

7. _____ tree frog is a kind of animal.

8. Put _____ orange and _____ pear in _____ blue basket on _____ table.

Parts of Speech Review

Circle nouns.
Cross out verbs.
Underline adjectives.

(food)

flower

~~jump~~

carry

fast

purple

purse

men

strong

cute

sing

hike

drive

tree

catch

happy

wet

family

climb

bicycle

sad

tall

build

school

Find the Words

who action when where

1. (the old lady)

2. [coughed]

3. tomorrow

4. near the bridge

5. Prince Charming

6. Mom and Dad

7. crept

8. pretty soon

9. at the party

10. scratched

11. a tired carpenter

12. one summer day

13. late last night

14. in the sky

15. around the corner

16. Mr. Barnum

17. knocked

18. rushed

©1995 by Evan-Moor Corp.

Language Fundamentals

Find the Words

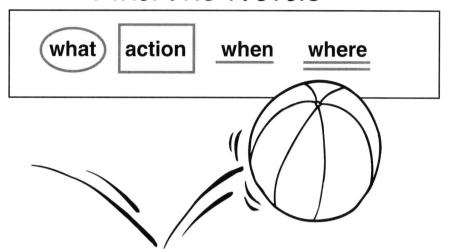

what | action | when | where

1. upstairs

2. caught

3. sniffed

4. in the cafeteria

5. skateboard

6. long ago

7. snored

8. over her head

9. garbage truck

10. after school

11. behind the cookie jar

12. spoke

13. when he was six

14. singing bird

15. in a bathtub

16. was cutting

17. someday

18. funny brown puppy

©1995 by Evan-Moor Corp.

Language Fundamentals

Who Did It?

The bird flew away today.

who   action   when   where

1. The city bus goes by my house every day.

2. The rooster on grandpa's farm crows at sunrise.

3. When it rains, my cat stays indoors.

4. The airplane for Kansas will leave at 10:30.

5. Each spring robins build nests in these trees.

6. A fire truck was parked there yesterday.

7. Just now a bumpy toad jumped into the pond.

8. That puppy always hides its bones in the backyard.

Adverbs

Adverbs tell *how, when, or where* something happens.

She walked **slowly** into the room.
He came **late**.
I saw her **there**.

Circle the **adverb** that tells about the underlined verb.

1. Mother <u>sang</u> quietly to the baby.

2. Jamal <u>played</u> in the backyard yesterday.

3. My cat <u>sat</u> right here.

4. Mr. Brown always <u>sails</u> his boat on the weekend.

5. Please <u>drive</u> carefully.

6. Milk <u>flew</u> everywhere when the carton broke.

7. Quickly Maggie <u>cleaned</u> it up.

8. Annie <u>waited</u> patiently for her turn.

How? When? Where?

Write **how**, **when**, or **where** after each adverb.

quietly _____   angrily _____

everywhere_____   always _____

late _____   yesterday_____

slowly _____   quickly _____

there _____   patiently _____

how...

when...

where...

Write a sentence using an adverb that tells when.

_____

_____

Write a sentence using an adverb that tells how.

_____

_____

Write a sentence using an adverb that tells where.

_____

_____

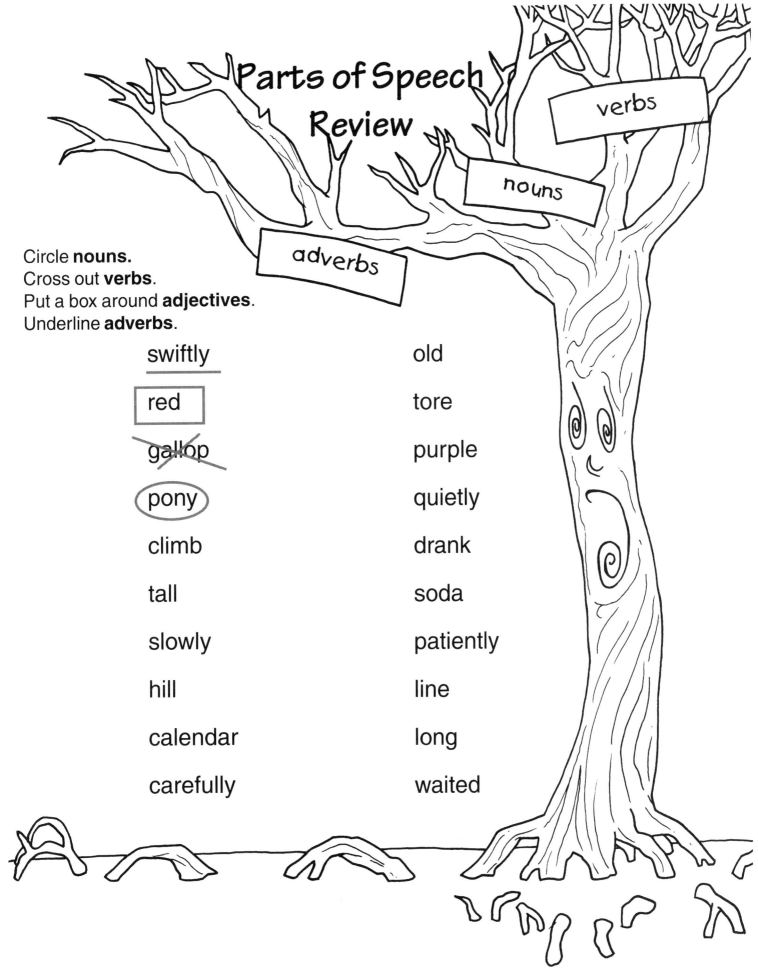

Parts of Speech Review

verbs

nouns

adverbs

Circle **nouns**.
Cross out **verbs**.
Put a box around **adjectives**.
Underline **adverbs**.

swiftly

red

gallop

pony

climb

tall

slowly

hill

calendar

carefully

old

tore

purple

quietly

drank

soda

patiently

line

long

waited

©1995 by Evan-Moor Corp.

Language Fundamentals

Subjects and Predicates

- **subject** - who or what the sentence is about
- **predicate** - what is said about the subject

"Find the Subject and Predicate"

Write short sentences on the chalkboard. Explain that students are going to tell you who or what the sentence is about (subject).

Point to each sentence one at a time. Have children read the sentence with you. Select someone to tell the subject. Have the child come up and underline that part in red.

Explain that now they are going to look for what is happening (predicate) in each sentence. Point to the sentences one at a time. Select someone to tell the predicate. Have the child come up and underline that part in green.

"Match the Parts to Make a Sentence"

Make a set of phrases on sentence strips. Have the subject of sentences on half of the strips and the predicate of sentences on the other half. Go through the strips with your students to be sure they can read the phrases. Pass the strips out.

Call one person to the front of the group to read his/her sentence out loud. Have everyone else read their phrases to see who has the other half of the sentence. Have that person come up and stand with the first person. Have them read their parts of the sentence aloud and tell if it is the subject or the predicate.

"Missing Predicates"

Write subjects on the board. Have students make up the predicates. Write these on the chalkboard also. Ask students to copy their favorite sentence and illustrate it. Do the same with predicates.

Select samples from the children's own writings for some of your examples.

Observe how children use language in their daily speech and in their own writings. This will help you determine who needs what type of practice.

Who or What?

Put a line under who or what the sentence is about.

1. <u>Ann and Kim</u> had a pet cat.

2. The red bike was for sale.

3. A fast train ran down the track.

4. My mom and dad like to swim.

5. Carlos went to see his grandmother.

6. The old dog was sleeping in the shade.

7. We like hot dogs and chips.

8. Texas is a big state.

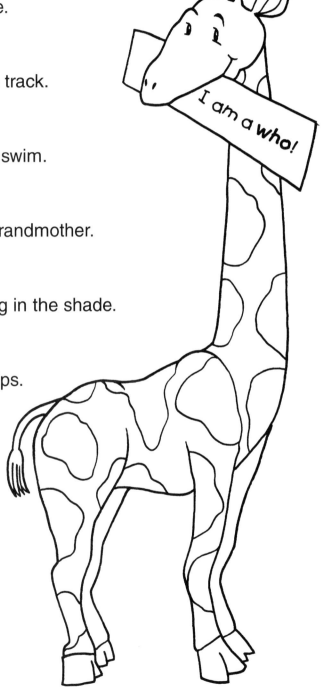

What Happened?

Put a circle around what happened in the sentence.

1. Bob and Sam (want a pet dog.)

2. The green sled went down the hill.

3. A fast boy ran on the sand at the beach.

4. My mom and dad like to play cards.

5. Carlos went to the store for his mother.

6. The old man sat on a bench in the park.

7. Can we have hamburgers for lunch?

8. Do you like to paint?

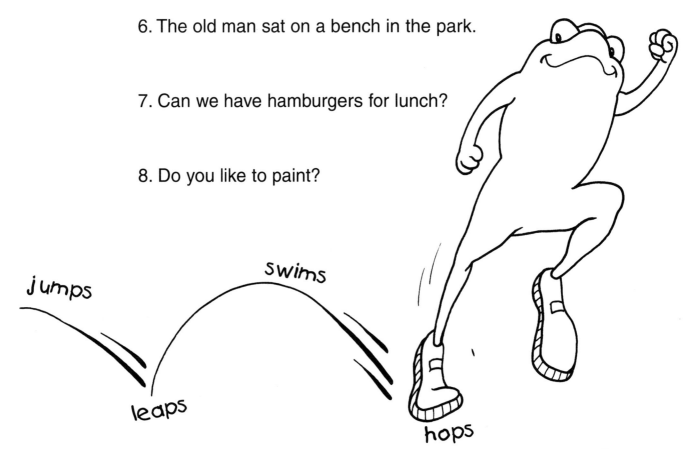

jumps

leaps

swims

hops

Subject and Predicate

Every sentence has two main parts:

subject - tells who or what the sentence is about

predicate - tells what the subject does.

Draw a line under the subject and a circle around the predicate.

1. Everyone in the class cheered.

2. The yellow bus went down the street.

3. The police took care of the people.

4. Jose fed the cat and dog.

5. The horses ran across the field.

6. The teacher liked my story.

7. I had to go to the dentist today.

8. Mrs. Brown made a birthday cake for Kim.

Who or What

The baby... cried
laughed
ate
crawled

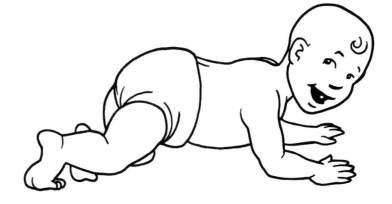

Add the subject to tell who or what the sentence is about.

1. _____ went to town.

2. _____ went into the barn.

3. _____ won the game.

4. _____ put out the fire.

5. _____ swam in the pond.

6. _____ landed on the roof.

7. _____ had pizza for lunch.

8. _____ planted bean seeds.

Answer Key

Part Two

Page 72
1. girl, apple, banana, sandwich
2. book, man, building
3. park, Boston
4. train, day, week, snow
5. cat, kittens, garage
6. helicopter, field, house

Page 77
1. teeth
   tooth
2. children
   child
3. mouse
   mice
4. geese
   goose
5. woman
   women

Page 79
1. foxes
2. cherries
3. buses
4. toys
5. bushes
6. puppies
7. stories
8. guesses

Page 81
1. boys'
2. pet's
3. baby's
4. bunnies'
5. parents'
6. bird's
7. artist's
8. boys'

Page 82
1. Uncle Ned's
2. Jamal, Tanisha, Wilson Street
3. Lake Louise, British Columbia
4. Mr. Garcia, Tijuana, Mexico
5. Dr. Brown
6. Paul, Angela
7. Mom, Dad, San Francisco, Sunday
8. Lee, Stan, Ollie

Page 83
Answers will vary.

Page 84
proper nouns are in **bold**
1. **Marcos**, soccer, **Saturday**
2. **Sally, Texas**, grandfather
3. **Mississippi River**, states
4. **Tony**, book, **Hiawatha**
5. duck, **Miller's Pond**
6. children, **Kyle's** party
7. squirrels, trees, **Elm Boulevard**
8. **Mark**, father, car

Page 85
1. he
2. we
3. she
4. it

Page 86
1. She, it
2. She, it
3. He, it
4. He, it

Page87
Pronouns are underlined.
1. sun, It
2. Sam, Ollie, They
3. Pete, I, We
4. Mr. Green, park, He, park
5. Ann, school, *She*, school

Page 88
1. she
2. it
3. it
4. he
5. we
6. he

Page 89
1. his
2. their
3. your
4. our
5. her
6. its

Page 90
1. them
2. them
3. her
4. him
5. it
6. us
7. him
8. her
9. them
10. us
11. them
12. it

Page 91
1. I
2. me
3. I
4. me

1. me
2. me
3. me
4. me

Page 97
1. is
2. are
3. is
4. are
5. are
6. are

Page 98
1. was
2. were
3. were
4. was
5. was
6. were

Page 99
1. runs, run
2. hop, hops
3. rides, ride
4. nap, naps

Page 100
1. jumping, jumped
2. hopped, hopping
3. looking, looked
4. played, playing

Page 101
1. fixes
2. hurries
3. tries
4. reaches
5. dries
6. rushes
7. fries
8. washes
9. mixes
10. passes
11. boxes
12. marries

Page 102
1. came
2. ran
3. gone
4. saw
5. seen
6. come
7. went
8. run

Page 103
give-gave
break-broke
begin-began
come-came
drive-drove
eat-ate
sleep-slept
grow-grew

Page 104
1. had
2. have
3. has
4. have
5. had
6. has
7. have
8. have

Page 105

1. looked 2. waited
3. stayed 4. walked
5. jumped 6. laughed
7. liked

Page 106

1. are 2. was
3. were 4. Were
5. am 6. is

Page 107

1. were
2. are
3. is
4. was
5. am
6. be
7. was
8. were

Page 113

six bugs
a brown hen
a cold snack
a big box
as happy smile

Page 114

fat, funny, hot, sleepy, fast
yellow, big, long, soft
busy, tall, red, old

Page 115

1. busy, fast
2. tired, wooden
3. big, yellow, cool
4. only, small
5. happy, shiny, new, big
6. frisky, green

Page 116

1. a an
2. the
3. an, a
4. a, the
5. an
6. The
7. A
8. an, a, the, the

Page 117

nouns:
food, flower, purse, men, tree, family, bicycle, school

verbs:
jump, carry, sing, hike, drive, catch, climb, build

adjectives:
fast, purple, strong, cute, happy, wet, sad, tall

Page 118

1. who 10. action
2. action 11. who
3. when 12. when
4. where 13. when
5. who 14. where
6. who 15. where
7. action 16. who
8. when 17. action
9. where 18. action

Page119

1. where 10. when
2. action 11. where
3. action 12. action
4. where 13. when
5. what 14. what
6. when 15. where
7. action 16. action
8. where 17. when
9. what 18. what

Page 120

	who	action	when	where
1.	city bus	goes	every day	by my house
2.	rooster	crows	at sunrise	on grandpa's farm
3.	my cat	stays	indoors	when it rains
4.	airplane	will leave	at 10:30	for Kansas
5.	robins	build nests	each spring	in these trees
6.	fire truck	was parked	yesterday	there
7.	bumpy toad	jumped	just now	into the pond
8.	that puppy	hides	always	in the backyard

Page 121

1. quietly
2. yesterday
3. here
4. always
5. carefully
6. everywhere
7. quickly
8. patiently

Page 122

how
where
when
how
where

how
when
when
how
how

Page 123

nouns	verbs	adjectives	adverbs
pony	gallop	red	swiftly
hill	climb	tall	slowly
calendar	tore	old	carefully
soda	drank	purple	quietly
line	waited	long	patiently

Page 125

1. Ann and Kim
2. The red bike
3. A fast train
4. My mom and dad
5. Carlos
6. The old dog
7. We
8. Texas

Page 126

1. want a pet dog
2. went down the hill
3. ran on the sand
4. like to play cards
5. went to the store
6. sat on a bench
7. have hamburgers for lunch
8. like to paint

Page 127

1. **Everyone in the class** - cheered
2. **The yellow bus** - went down the street
3. **The police** - took care of the people
4. **Jose** - fed the cat and dog
5. **The horses** - ran across the field
6. **The teacher** - liked my story
7. **I** - had to go to the dentist today
8. **Mrs. Brown** - made a birthday cake for Kim

Page 128

Answers will vary.

The **Answer Key** for this section is found on pages 189-190

Section
Three

Other Language Skills

What is included in this section?

- Changing words to new forms: *(page 135)*
    - Compound Words
    - Abbreviations
    - Contractions

- Increasing Vocabulary: *(page 157)*
    - Words with the same or similar meanings (synonyms)
    - Words with opposite meanings (antonyms)
    - Words which sound the same but are spelled differently and have different meanings (homophones)

- Alphabetical Order: *(page 175)*
    - what it is
    - alphabetizing by - letters, words
    - when we use it - dictionary
                        telephone book
                        library

Using the pages in this section:

When selecting pages to use with your students, consider which areas they need to practice and at what level that practice needs to be. The variety of pages available for use allows you to individualize practice activities to better meet your students' needs.

At the simplest level students identify pictures and group them by type (nouns, compound words, etc.), put letters in alphabetical order, and recognize some compound words and contractions.

At the highest level students are required to identify parts of speech, write words with new endings, alphabetize words through the second letter, use alphabetizing skills to locate information, etc.

Group and Center Activities

Many of the sets of cards can be used to play "Find My Match." Reproduce the appropriate set of cards and follow these directions. You will find cards on these pages:

Pages 137-144 **Compound Words, Contractions, Abbreviations**
Pages 158-163 **Synonyms, Antonyms, Homophones**

"Find My Match"
Reproduce the cards. Pass them out among your students. Have one child come up to the front of the group and show his/her card. Ask "Who has a word that_____?" When all cards have been collected, go through the whole stack reading the pairs.

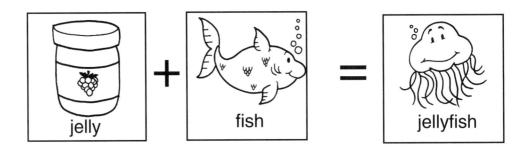

"Center Fun"
Put the same cards in a center for partner or individual practice of the skill.

"I Read It in the Newspaper"
Any type of word you are studying can become the topic for a Newspaper Search. Give partners a page from the newspaper. Name the topic (compound words, abbreviations, etc.). Allow a set amount of time for students to see how many words they can find and circle.

Changing Words to New Forms

- Compound Words
- Abbreviations
- Contractions

"Word + Word = New Word"

Use the cards (pages137-140). Show the cards to be sure students can identify the picture or read the words. Pass the cards out to your students. Call up two students at a time to show their cards. Have them put the cards together to see if they make a real word. If the words do form a compound word, write it on a chart. Have each student select one or more of the compound words to illustrate. (The illustrations could be put in a cover to make a class book titled "Compound Words."

"Take it Away"

Help children understand that you can create new words by removing letters and adding an apostrophe. Write a word on board. Ask "What do we take away?" Erase letter/letters. Add the apostrophe in colored chalk. Do several together to model the process, then write a list of words on the board (select those appropriate for your students). Call children up one at a time to change a word into a contraction. When the list is complete, challenge students to use each word in an oral sentence.

cannot   **cannot**   **can't**

We can't go outside to play.

"Who am I?"

Show an abbreviation card (example - Dr.). Ask "Who is this?" After the students identify the abbreviation, show the card for the complete word. When you have gone through all of the abbreviations, write a series of names with titles on the chalkboard. Select children to read them.

Doctor	Dr.

"Find My Abbreviation"

Write a list of words on the chalkboard. Write a second list containing the abbreviations next to the first list. Go through each word to be sure your students can read them.
Call students up one at a time to draw a line between the word and its abbreviation.

Sunday	Sun

"Which is It?"

Place the contraction and abbreviation cards in a center for partner or individual practice in identifying which is a contraction and which is an abbreviation.

cannot	can't

Note: Reproduce these **compound word picture cards** to use with group and center activities.

cow	**boy**	**cowboy**
nut	**cracker**	**nutcracker**
rain	**bow**	**rainbow**
basket	**ball**	**basketball**

©1995 by Evan-Moor Corp.   Language Fundamentals

dragon | fly | dragonfly

jelly | fish | jellyfish

cup | cake | cupcake

skate | board | skateboard

sun	flower	**sunflower**
day	dream	**daydream**
butter	fly	**butterfly**
earth	quake	**earthquake**
gold	fish	**goldfish**

motor	cycle	**motorcycle**
water	melon	**watermelon**
rattle	snake	**rattlesnake**
touch	down	**touchdown**

cannot	do not
will not	I will
it is	we are
I have	what is
I am	did not

can't	don't
won't	I'll
it's	we're
I've	what's
I'm	didn't

Doctor	Professor
Mister	Sunday
inch	December
pound	New York
Reverend	quart

Dr.	**Prof.**
Mr.	**Sun.**
in.	**Dec.**
lb.	**NY**
Rev.	**qt.**

Making Big Words

Write the compound words.   Draw pictures of the new words.

rain + bow =

_____

_ _ _ _ _ _ _ _ _ _ _ _ _ _ _

_____

cup + cake =

_____

_ _ _ _ _ _ _ _ _ _ _ _ _ _ _

_____

basket + ball =

_____

_ _ _ _ _ _ _ _ _ _ _ _ _ _ _

_____

jelly + fish =

_____

_ _ _ _ _ _ _ _ _ _ _ _ _ _ _

_____

skate + board =

_____

_ _ _ _ _ _ _ _ _ _ _ _ _ _ _

_____

gold + fish =

_____

_ _ _ _ _ _ _ _ _ _ _ _ _ _ _

_____

Compound Words

Circle the compound words in each sentence.
Some sentences have more than one compound word.

1. We had applesauce with our pork chops for dinner last night.

2. Did you feel that earthquake?

3. We rode the streetcar out to the airport.

4. My teacher doesn't like it when we daydream in class.

5. I caught a jellyfish on my hook when I was fishing at the wharf.

6. Our grandfather made a big bowl of popcorn for us to eat while we watched the football game.

List the compound words you found.

_____

_____

_____

_____

_____

_____

_____

_____

_____

_____

_____

_____

_____

Using Compound Words

cupcake	goldfish
skateboard	rainbow
cowboy	sunflower
basketball	butterfly

Fill in the blanks.

1. I have a _____ in my lunch box.

2. Did you get to play in the _____ game?

3. How many _____ are in that tank?

4. My mom planted a _____ in the backyard.

5. Can I have a _____ for my birthday?

6. Bob and Ted went to a _____ movie.

7. A yellow _____ sat on the flower.

8. A big _____ was high up in the sky.

©1995 by Evan-Moor Corp. Language Fundamentals

Making Contractions

is not -	**isn't**
cannot -	**can't**
do not -	**don't**

Write a contraction in the blank.

1. That _____ my cat.

2. Bob _____ find his kite.

3. We _____ want to go.

4. I _____ like snakes.

5. That _____ my cat.

6. Dad _____ go now.

7. Ken _____ here.

8. I _____ go to sleep.

Contractions

A contraction is a short way of writing a word.
An apostrophe is put where letters are taken away.

do not - **don't**   I will - **I'll**

Write the contraction for these words.

do not   _____

cannot   _____

would not   _____

is not   _____

I will   _____

he will   _____

they will   _____

she will   _____

he is   _____

what is   _____

it is   _____

that is   _____

Some words change a lot.

will not - **won't**

of the clock - **o'clock**

Contractions

Write the contraction in each sentence.

1. Mark _____ find his homework.
   (cannot)

2. It _____ in his backpack.
   (is not)

3. He looked in his room. It _____ in his room.
   (was not)

4. He needs to find it soon or _____ be late for school.
   (he will)

5. _____ ask Mother.
   (I will)

6. Maybe _____ know where it is.
   (she will)

is ...*isn†*

not

7. _____ on the kitchen table.
   (It is)

8. _____ better hurry. The bus is coming.
   (You had)

What's in the Contraction?

...you re

you are

Write the words that are in these contractions.

can't ___ cannot ___   I'm ___

isn't ___   didn't ___

I'll ___   you're ___

it's ___   let's ___

don't ___   I'd ___

haven't ___   that's ___

©1995 by Evan-Moor Corp.   Language Fundamentals

Abbreviations

Match.

Mon.   • Sunday

Fri.   • Monday

Sat.   • Tuesday

Sun.   • Wednesday

Wed.   • Thursday

Tues.   • Friday

Thurs.   • Saturday

An apple a day keeps the doctor away.

©1995 by Evan-Moor Corp.   152

Abbreviations
Months

January	May	September
February	June	October
March	July	November
April	August	December

Write the month. _____

Dec. _____

Oct. _____

Jan. _____

Sept. _____

Feb. _____

Aug. _____

Nov. _____

©1995 by Evan-Moor Corp.   Language Fundamentals

Abbreviations
People and Titles

Use a period after abbreviations.

Doctor - **Dr.**	Junior - **Jr.**
Governor - **Gov.**	Reverend - **Rev.**
Professor - **Prof.**	Captain - **Capt.**

Remember to punctuate these titles too.

Mr.

Ms.

Mrs.

Add periods where they are needed.

1. The pastor of our church is Rev Williams.

2. Dr Garcia took my temperature to see if I had a fever.

3. After the party, Mrs Adams took the children home.

4. Prof Martin taught our class yesterday.

5. Capt Smith has been in the army for a long time.

6. Jack Hamilton, Jr is the son of Gov Hamilton.

_____

Write two sentences using title abbreviations.
Don't forget to use capital letters and periods.

1. _____

_____

2. _____

_____

Abbreviation
Measurement

Match.

c.	tablespoon
cm	centimeter
lb.	cup
ft.	quart
km	pound
tsp.	kilometer
Tbsp.	Centigrade
oz.	foot
in.	pint
qt.	number
C	teaspoon
doz.	amount
gal.	ounce
pt.	yard
no.	dozen
yd.	gallon
amt.	inch

Match the Abbreviation

Doctor   Gov.

Mister   Prof.

Professor   Dr.

Governor   Capt.

Reverend   Mr.

Captain   Jr.

Junior   Rev.

©1995 by Evan-Moor Corp.   Language Fundamentals

Increasing Vocabulary

- **Synonyms** - words with the same or similar meanings
- **Antonyms** - words with opposite meanings
- **Homophones** - words which sound the same but are spelled differently and have different meanings

"Pick-a-Word, Make-a-Match"

Put half of the word cards (synonyms, antonyms, or homophones) along the chalk tray. Put their matching word cards in a paper sack. Call up a child to draw a card out of the bag. The child then tries to find its match among the words on the chalk tray.

"Show Me"

Reproduce a set of synonym cards for each child. Show a word to the class. Have children find its synonym to hold up when you say "Show me."

Now, write a series of sentences on the chalkboard or a plastic overlay. Underline a word in each sentence for which children are to find the synonym. Select a child to read a sentence out loud. Point to the underlined word. Children will hold up a synonym for the underlined word when you say "Show me." and have children find its synonym to hold up when you say "Show me." Select a child to erase the word and write the synonym. Have the class read the sentence again with its new word.

This activity can also be done using antonyms or homophones.

"Independent Practice"

Put a set of each type of cards in a center for children needing extra practice with any of the types of words.

Note: Reproduce these **synonym word cards** to use with group and center activities.

synonyms **big**	*synonyms* large
synonyms **little**	*synonyms* small
synonyms **look**	*synonyms* see
synonyms **start**	*synonyms* begin
synonyms **shut**	*synonyms* close

Note: Reproduce these **synonym word cards** to use with group and center activities.

synonyms **fast**	*synonyms* quick
synonyms **like**	*synonyms* enjoy
synonyms **go**	*synonyms* leave
synonyms **part**	*synonyms* piece
synonyms **huge**	*synonyms* vast

Note: Reproduce these **antonym word cards** to use with group and center activities.

antonyms **up**	*antonyms* down
antonyms **to**	*antonyms* from
antonyms **on**	*antonyms* off
antonyms **all**	*antonyms* none
antonyms **here**	*antonyms* there

©1995 by Evan-Moor Corp. Language Fundamentals

Note: Reproduce these **antonym word cards** to use with group and center activities.

antonyms	antonyms
slow	quick

antonyms	antonyms
ask	tell

antonyms	antonyms
part	whole

antonyms	antonyms
right	wrong

antonyms	antonyms
noisy	quiet

©1995 by Evan-Moor Corp.   Language Fundamentals

Note: Reproduce these **homophone word cards** to use with group and center activities.

homophone **to**	*homophone* two
homophone **ate**	*homophone* eight
homophone **blue**	*homophone* blew
homophone **flour**	*homophone* flower
homophone **brake**	*homophone* break

homophone

red

homophone

read

homophone

ant

homophone

aunt

homophone

beet

homophone

beat

homophone

die

homophone

dye

homophone

aloud

homophone

allowed

Note: You may want to introduce the term **synonym** at this time.

Words that Mean the Same

Match.

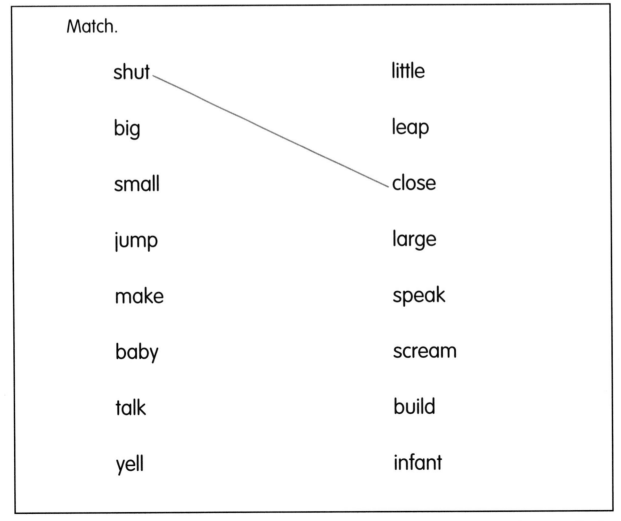

shut	little
big	leap
small	close
jump	large
make	speak
baby	scream
talk	build
yell	infant

Name the Picture

Write two words that name each picture.

Word Box

baby	infant	scream
bright	jump	shiny
build	leap	sick
ill	make	yell

Fill in the Blanks

Think about the underlined word.
Write a new word that means the same thing.

1. The <u>small</u> frog hopped into the pond. _____

2. I saw a <u>large</u> elephant at the zoo. _____

3. Did you hear the teacher <u>speak</u>? _____

4. Please <u>build</u> me a swing. _____

5. Don't <u>scream</u>, the baby is asleep. _____

6. Please <u>close</u> the door. _____

little	hard	big
make	leap	yell
shut	talk	fast

Opposites

Draw these opposites.

in out	big little
happy sad	hot cold
dirty clean	asleep awake

©1995 by Evan-Moor Corp. Language Fundamentals

Match Opposites

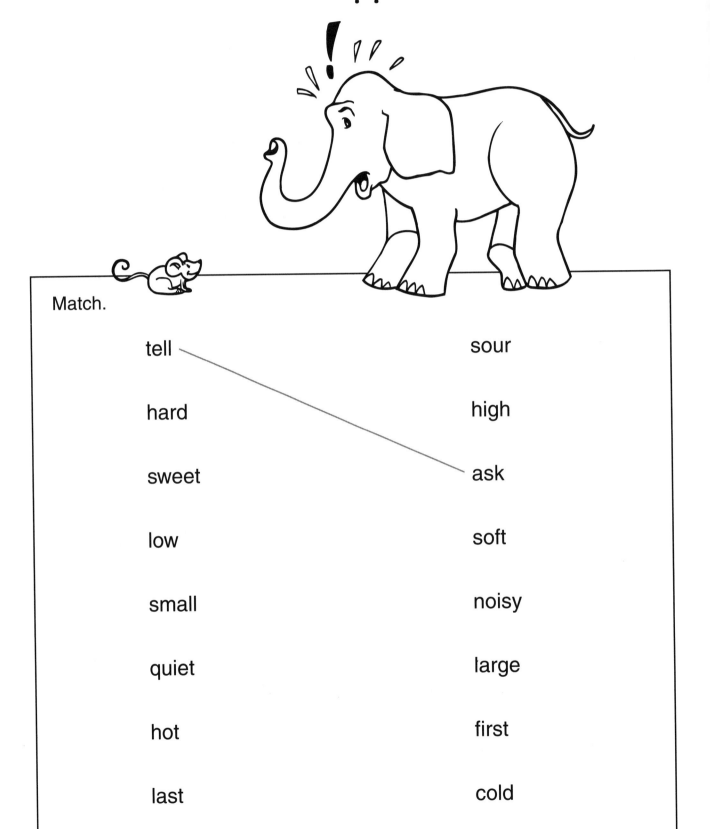

Match.

tell   sour

hard   high

sweet   ask

low   soft

small   noisy

quiet   large

hot   first

last   cold

Using Opposites

Look at the underlined word.
Write a word that means the opposite.

1. The man was carrying a <u>heavy</u> box.   <u>light</u>

2. I <u>lost</u> my homework.

3. The clown had a <u>sad</u> face.

4. We rode the train all <u>day</u> .

5. Did you put on <u>dirty</u> socks?

6. My baby sister is <u>awake</u> in her crib.

7. The wooden chair was <u>bumpy</u>.

8. How <u>slow</u> did you walk?

©1995 by Evan-Moor Corp.   Language Fundamentals

Words that Sound Alike

Write the right word on the line.

ant - aunt

1. My _____aunt_____ likes to sing.

   An _____ant_____ was in the candy jar.

beat - beet

2. I _____ my friend at chess.

   Mom planted _____ seeds in the garden.

ate - eight

3. Carlos will be _____ on his birthday.

   He _____ pizza for dinner.

break - brake

4. I need a new _____ on my bike.

   Did you _____ my new toy?

blew - blue

5. The wind _____ all day.

   My new skateboard is _____.

fir - fur

6. Dad cut down the _____ tree in our back yard.

   My dog got mud in his _____ rolling in the puddle.

Homophones

Homophones sound the same, but are not spelled the same and do not mean the same thing.

bow

bough

Match.

by	bough
eye	flower
berry	buy
bow	I
flour	bury
doe	flea
cheap	scent
flee	allowed
cent	cheep
aloud	dough

©1995 by Evan-Moor Corp.
Language Fundamentals

Homophones

Circle the right word.

1. Do you (know no) how to make your lunch?

2. I read a story about a brave (night knight).

3. Dad put a new (pane pain) of glass in the window.

4. Tim didn't (know no) the way to the store.

5. May I have a (peace piece) of pie?

6. How many (rose rows) of beans did you plant?

7. We had to wait an (our hour) to catch the bus.

8. Did you eat the (hole whole) pizza?

©1995 by Evan-Moor Corp. Language Fundamentals

Words that Sound the Same

Write the right word on each line.

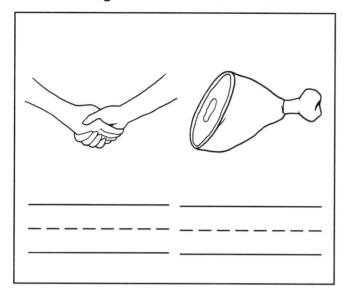

_____ _____

- - - - - - - - - - - - - - - - - - - - - -

_____ _____

_____ _____

- - - - - - - - - - - - - - - - - - - - - -

_____ _____

_____ _____

- - - - - - - - - - - - - - - - - - - - - -

_____ _____

_____ _____

- - - - - - - - - - - - - - - - - - - - - -

_____ _____

Word Box

bawl	ball
hair	hare
meat	meet
one	won

©1995 by Evan-Moor Corp.

Language Fundamentals

To, Two, or Too?

to - in the direction of
too - also or more than enough
two - a number

Write **to**, **too**, or **two** in each sentence.

1. I am going _____ see my friend.

2. My little sister is _____ years old.

3. Can I go _____?

4. We have _____ bathrooms in our new house.

5. I ate _____ much cake.

6. Will you go _____ the zoo with me?

I am two.

Me too.

Write sentences.

two 1. _____

to 2. _____

too 3. _____

Alphabetical Order

- what it is
- alphabetizing by - letters, words
- when we use it - dictionary
                   telephone book
                   library

"What Letter Comes Next?"

Make a set of letter cards (pages 17-19). Mix up the cards. Show one card at a time, asking "What comes next?" Go through the whole alphabet. (A more challenging version of this activity is played by asking what letter comes before.)

Pass out all of the cards. Ask students to come up with their cards and line up in the correct ABC order.

"Put the Words in Order"

Practice alphabetical order by the first letter. Write the letters of the alphabet in order on the chalkboard. Make a set of word cards (or use cards from the previous sections). Show two word cards at a time. Call up two students and give each a card. Have the students hold their word cards by the letter with which they begin. Ask the class to tell you which word comes first in the alphabet. (Use three cards, then more, as students become more proficient.)

ape	ball	cup

"Look at the Second Letter"

Write the letters of the alphabet on the chalkboard to use as a reference point as you follow these directions. Write a list of words (start with two or three) on the chalkboard. Have a student underline, in color, the letter that is the same in each word. Have a second child underline the next letter of each word in a second color. Ask students to decide the alphabetical order of words.

Alphabetical Order Activities

Dictionary Activities

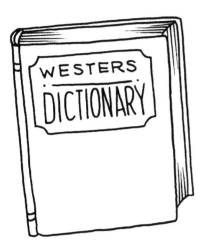

Use these alphabetical order activities with students who are reading and have had an introduction to finding words in a dictionary. Have students work in pairs or individually.

"Where Is It?"
Put the alphabet on the chalkboard, writing the letters in three sections.

> beginning - a b c d e f g h i
> middle - j k l m n o p q
> end - r s t u v w x y z

Show a word card. Ask students to tell you if the word would be found in the beginning, middle, or end of the dictionary.

"Dictionary Search"
Show a word card (or write a word on the chalkboard) and have students see how fast they can locate it in the dictionary. When the word is found, students are to raise their hands. Call on someone to give the page number on which he/she found the word.

Telephone Book Activities

"Find Your Name"
Collect some old telephone books. Show students how to locate a name in the telephone book using alphabetical order. Have each child locate his/her own last name and count how many times the name is listed.

Challenge older students to locate a store, business, movie theater, etc., in the yellow pages by using alphabetical order.

Library Activities

"Alphabet Search"
Take your class on an alphabet search in the library. See how many places they can find where the alphabet is used to help people locate books or information.

What Is Missing?

Cut and paste the missing letters in order.

		a		c
	e		g	
i		k	l	m
	o	p	q	
s	t			w
x		z		

j	u	d	n	v
r	b	h	y	f

Alphabet Puzzle

Paste the puzzle together.

Cut out the pieces.

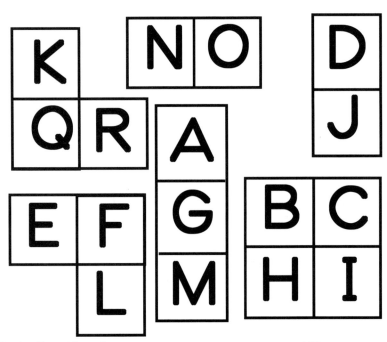

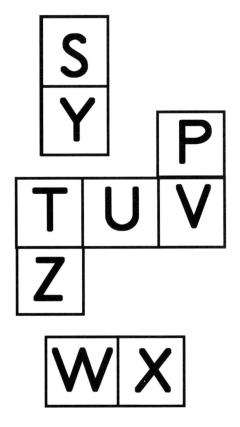

©1995 by Evan-Moor Corp.

Language Fundamentals

Alphabetical order

Write the words in alphabetical order.

1. _____

| dog | bug | cat |

2. _____

| Ron | Ted | Sam |

3. _____

| nut | on | map |

4. _____

| egg | gum | fat |

5. _____

| hat | jam | ink |

©1995 by Evan-Moor Corp. Language Fundamentals

Balloon Fun

Put the words in alphabetical order.
Color the balloons.

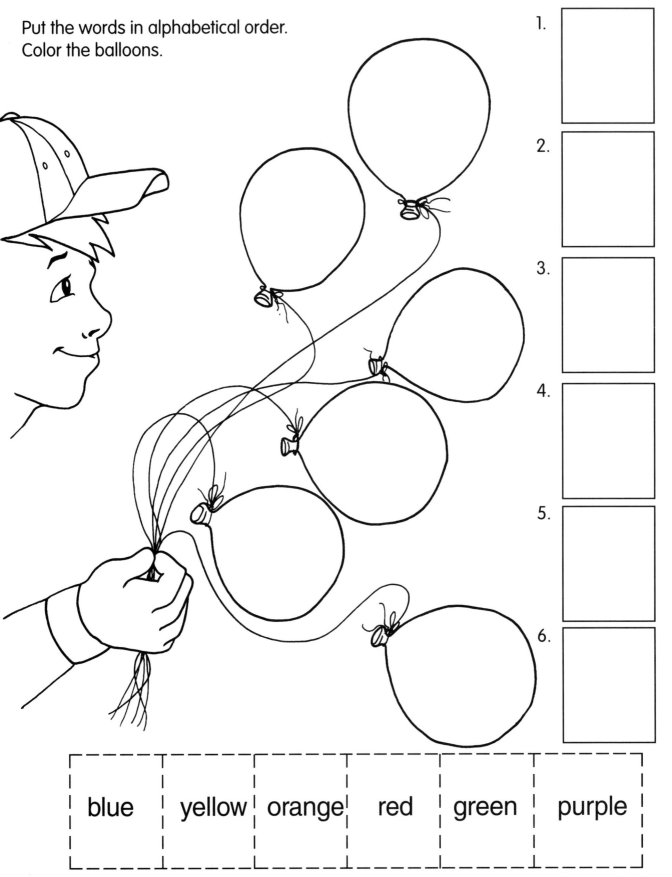

1.

2.

3.

4.

5.

6.

| blue | yellow | orange | red | green | purple |

Dot-to-Dot

Connect the dots.
Color the picture.

• **can**

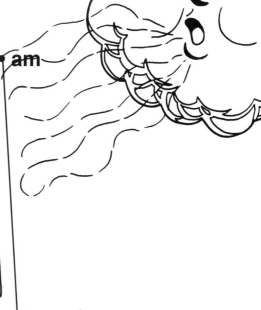

• **am**

• **fun**

• **is**

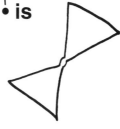

• **no**

• **ran**

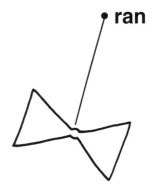

Write the words in alphabetical order.

1. _____

2. _____

3. _____

4. _____

5. _____

6. _____

©1995 by Evan-Moor Corp.   181   Language Fundamentals

Alphabetical Toys

Write the toys in alphabetical order.

1. _____

2. _____

3. _____

4. _____

5. _____

6. _____

7. _____

8. _____

9. _____

10. _____

11. _____

12. _____

Toy Box

jeep	tank	airplane
trunk	ball	kite
bike	wagon	doll
top	van	car

Follow the Dots

Connect the dots and color.

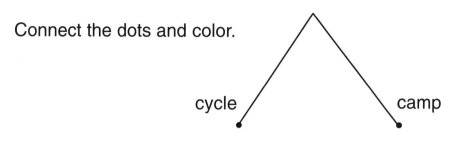

cycle

camp

•cent

cut •

crisp •

• chair

• clean

clean

• cot

• circus

cot

circus

Write the words in order.

1._____   6._____

2._____   7._____

3._____   8._____

4._____   9._____

5._____

©1995 by Evan-Moor Corp.   Language Fundamentals

Sort It Out

Put the words in alphabetical order.

1. _____
2. _____
3. _____
4. _____

1. _____
2. _____
3. _____
4. _____

elephant

egg

ears

eel

squirrel

skates

shoe

store

PETS

An ABC Challenge

1. _____
2. _____
3. _____

cat

can

cap

1. _____
2. _____
3. _____

grin

grunt

grass

1. _____
2. _____
3. _____

stamp

stop

step

©1995 by Evan-Moor Corp.

Language Fundamentals

Look Carefully

Look at the second letter.
Write the letters in alphabetical order.

cat

1. _____

2. _____

at   am

1. _____

2. _____

get   got

1. _____

2. _____

hot   hit

1. _____

2. _____

3. _____

cup cap cot

1. _____

2. _____

3. _____

ham   hug   his

1. _____

2. _____

3. _____

pen pin pan

©1995 by Evan-Moor Corp.

Language Fundamentals

For Superstars Only

1. _____

2. _____

3. _____

4. _____

1. _____

2. _____

3. _____

4. _____

1. _____

2. _____

3. _____

4. _____

door	three	man
down	that	mad
dog	this	mat
doll	the	map

©1995 by Evan-Moor Corp.

Language Fundamentals

Alphabet Scramble

Write the words in alphabetical order to make sentences.

_____

1. _____

pretty	Ann	is

_____

2. _____

Dad	work	to	has

_____

3. _____

fat	hops	frog	A

_____

4. _____

play	Can	he	you	with

_____

5. _____

stopped	Sam	train	toy	the

Answer Key

Part Three

Page 146
1. applesauce
2. earthquake
3. streetcar, airport
4. daydream
5. jellyfish
6. grandfather, popcorn, football

Page 147
1. cupcake
2. basketball
3. goldfish
4. sunflower, backyard
5. skateboard
6. cowboy
7. butterfly
8. rainbow

Page 148
1. isn't
2. can't
3. don't
4. don't
5. isn't
6. can't
7. isn't
8. can't

Page 149
don't
can't
wouldn't
isn't
I'll
he'll
they'll
she'll
he's
what's
it's
that's

Page 150
1. can't
2. isn't
3. wasn't
4. he'll
5. I'll
6. she'll
7. It's
8. You'd

Page 151
cannot
is not
I will
it is
do not
have not
I am
did not
you are
let us
I would
that is

Page 154
1. Rev.
2. Dr.
3. Mrs.
4. Prof.
5. Capt.
6. Jr., Gov.

Page 155
c.= 1 cup
cm=centimeter
lb.=pound
ft.=foot
km=kilometer
tsp.=teaspoon
Tbsp.=tablespoon
oz.=ounce
in.=inch
qt.=quart
C=Centigrade
doz.=dozen
gal.=gallon
pt.=pint
no.=number
yd.=yard
amt.=amount

Page 156
Doctor=Dr.
Mister=Mr.
Professor=Prof.
Governor=Gov.
Reverend=Rev.
Captain=Capt.
Junior=Jr.

Page 164
shut-close
big-large
small-little
jump-leap
make-build
baby-infant
talk-speak
yell-scream

Page 165
scream-yell
baby-infant
ill-sick
jump-leap

Page 166
1. small-little
2. large-big
3. speak-talk
4. build-make
5. scream-yell
6. close-shut

Page 168
tell-ask
hard-soft
sweet-sour
low-high
small-large
quiet-noisy
hot-cold
last-first

Page 169
1. light
2. found
3. happy
4. night
5. dirty-clean
6. awake-asleep
7. bumpy-smooth
8. slow-fast

©1995 by Evan-Moor Corp.

Language Fundamentals

Page 170
1. aunt
   ant
2. beat
   beet
3. eight
   ate
4. brake
   break
5. blew
   blue
6. fir
   fur

Page 171
by-buy
eye-I
berry-bury
bow-bough
flour-flower
dow-dough
cheap-cheep
flee-flea
cent-scent
aloud-allowed

Page 172
1. know
2. knight
3. pane
4. know
5. piece
6. rows
7. hour
8. whole

Page 173
meet-meat
won-one
ball-bawl
hare-hair

Page 174
1. to
2. two
3. too
4. two
5. too
6. to

Page 179
1. bug, cat, dog
2. Ron, Sam Ted
3. map, nut on
4. egg, fat, gum
5. hat, ink, jam

Page 180
1. blue
2. green
3. orange
4. purple
5. red
6. yellow

Page 181
1. am
2. can
3. fun
4. is
5. no
6. ran

Page 182
1. airplane
2. ball
3. bike
4. bus
5. car
6. doll
7. jeep
8. kite
9. sailboat
10. tank
11. top
12. trunk
13. wagon
14. van
15. wagon

Page 183
1. camp
2. cent
3. chair
4. circus
5. clean
6. cot
7. crisp
8. cut

Page 184
ears, eel, egg, elephant
shoe, skates, squirrel, store

Page 185
1. can
2. can
3. cap
1. grass
2. grin
3. grunt
1. stamp
2. step
3. stop

Page 186
1. am
2. at
1. get
2. got
1. hit
2. hot
1. cap
2. cot
3. cup
1. ham
2. his
3. hug
1. pan
2. pin
3. pen

Page 187
dog, doll, door, down
that, the, this three
man, mad, map, mat

Page 188
1. Ann is pretty.
2. Dad has to work.
3. A fat frog hops.
4. Can he play with you?
5. Sam stopped the toy train.

The **Answer Key** for this section is found on page 240.

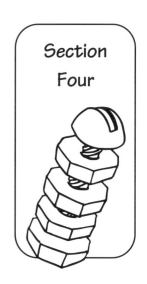

Written Language

What do we mean by "written language"?
Whatever we can think or say can be communicated to others using the symbols we call letters and words. This written communication can be as simple as a word, phrase, or sentence or as complex as a story or report.

What is included in this section?
- Sentences *(page 196)*
    - complete sentences
    - sentence patterns
    - super sentences
- Paragraphs *(page 207)*
    - parts of a paragraph
    - types of paragraphs
- Stories *(page 219)*
    - parts of a story
    - planning a story
- Editing *(page 231)*
    - editing checklist
    - proofreader marks (introduction)
- Publishing *(page 236)*
    - group and individual books
    - illustrations
    - covers for stories

Using the pages in this section:
When selecting pages to use with your students, consider which areas they need to practice and at what level that practice needs to be. The variety of pages available for use allows you to individualize practice activities to better meet your students' needs.

At the simplest level there are pages asking children to write simple sentences.

At the highest level, students are asked to write a complete story.

Preparation for Activities

Before Writing

Before beginning any independent writing activity it is important to prepare your students by doing some prewriting activities.

1. Keep in mind your students' needs and skill level when planning writing assignments. Some first graders may be ready for longer stories while some third graders may still be having difficulty writing interesting sentences.

2. Be sure the writer is familiar with the type of writing he/she is being asked to do. Whether it is a simple sentence, a paragraph, or a complete story, students need to hear many examples before writing their own. Read examples from literature and point out examples in their own oral and written expressions.

3. Model the writing task. This is important even for children at the prewriting level. They need to see that what is thought or said can be written down and read back.

Guide students through as many practice sessions as are necessary to prepare them for the independent writing task.

4. Brainstorm with students to develop lists of both ideas to write about and words to use in that writing. This is especially important for children who lack confidence or who have a limited background of experiences and language.

5. Share completed writings with the whole class. You can post these on a bulletin board, make collections into group or class books, or "publish" individual stories.

Word Banks

Pages 193-195 contain word banks. These words can be written on large charts and posted in the room for student use, or they can be reproduced for students to keep in their writing folders. Add words to the lists as they are requested by students. Seeing a wide variety of words can stimulate ideas and encourage rich use of language in both oral and written expression.

Word Bank

Words that Name
(nouns)

people	places	animals	things
astronaut	backyard	beetle	bicycle
boy	beach	butterfly	carousel
clown	cabin	dragon	chair
cowboy	castle	elephant	door
dancer	city	giraffe	flower
doctor	country	gorilla	fruit
father	desert	horse	hammer
fire fighter	field	hummingbird	ladder
giant	fort	monkey	pickle
girl	gym	octopus	pumpkin
inventor	home	pelican	shuttle
king	library	python	telephone
mother	mountain	robin	train
pilot	ocean	shark	truck
prince	park	unicorn	vegetable
princess	school	walrus	waffle
queen	stadium	whale	wagon
teacher	zoo	wolf	xylophone

Word Bank

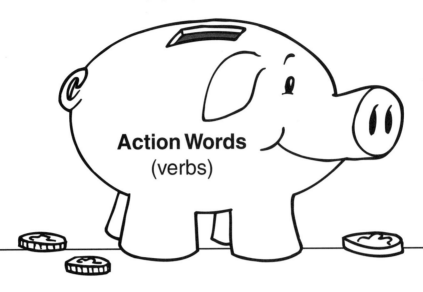

Action Words
(verbs)

argue	gallop	race
ask	help	rescue
build	hike	repair
call	invent	return
capture	laugh	roll
chase	leap	search
clean	leave	shout
climb	operate	sing
cook	paint	sleep
cry	plant	speak
dance	play	swim
discover	peek	take
draw	pray	tumble
drive	pretend	wash

©1995 by Evan-Moor Corp.   Language Fundamentals

Word Bank

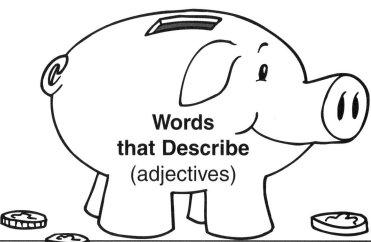

**Words
that Describe**
(adjectives)

			Colors
angry	fast	round	
awful	funny	sharp	**Colors**
beautiful	furry	short	black
big	grumpy	slimy	blue
broken	happy	slippery	gray
bumpy	hard	slow	green
busy	hot	smooth	orange
clean	huge	soft	pink
cold	lazy	sour	purple
colorful	little	sticky	red
cool	long	straight	tan
curly	narrow	sweet	white
cute	new	tall	yellow
damp	noisy	tasty	
dirty	old	tiny	
dry	quiet	ugly	
dull	ragged	warm	
dusty	rotten	wrinkled	

Sentences

- complete sentences
- sentence patterns
- super sentences

Sentence Patterns

Practice simple sentence patterns on the chalkboard with the whole class or small groups.

Noun - Verb:

Put your name on the board. Have students tell what actions you could take. List these next to your name.

> Mrs. Gomez talks.
> _____ reads
> _____ give directions
> _____ laughs

Now erase your name and ask "Who else can (name one of the activities listed) ?" Write names in front of the action as they are given.

> Sally talks.
> The librarian reads.
> Coach gives directions.
> Pedro laughs.

Noun - Verb - Noun:

Put a simple NVN sentence on the board. Have students read it, then proceed to change each element with their help.

> Bob ate pizza.
> Bob ate popcorn.
> Bob ate yogurt.
>
> Sally played ball.
> Sally kicked a ball.
> Sally threw a ball.
>
> The dog was funny.
> The clown was funny.
> The monkey was funny.

Noun - Verb - Adverb:
Put a noun and verb on the board. Ask students to provide a word telling how the action was done (an adverb).

The pony ran _____.
quickly
noisily
slowly

Super Sentences

This process can be used with young writers just beginning to put their words on paper and for experienced writers who need to learn ways of making sentences more interesting.

At the modeling level, begin with a set simple sentences. For example, The dog sleeps. Write this sentence on the chalkboard. Draw the following chart on the chalkboard also. You may use as many or as few sections as are suitable for your students.

describing words	who or what	did what?	where?	why?
The	dog	sleeps		

1. Brainstorm one category at a time beginning with describing words. List children's suggestions.

2. Allow time for children to create many oral sentences using just the basic sentence plus describing words.

The fat dog sleeps.
The furry dog sleeps.
The lazy brown dog sleeps.

3. Follow steps 1 and 2 to fill in the other columns, including other words for dog and other actions a dog might do. Do only those columns that are appropriate for your students.

4. Have children write sentences using words from each column.

You might have students see how many different sentences they can write, or have them write one "super sentence" and illustrate it. These pages can be put together in covers to make group picture books.

Pages 198-206 contain some sentence writing activities you can reproduce for the whole class or for individual students needing a bit more help.

Super Sentence

Write a super sentence about a dog. Tell...

1. what the dog looks like
2. what the dog is doing
3. where the dog is doing it

zzz

_____

- -

_____

_____

_____

- -

_____

_____

_____

- -

_____

_____

_____

- -

_____

Draw the dog here.

Super Sentence

Write a super sentence about a shark. Tell...

1. what the shark looks like
2. what the shark is doing
3. where the shark is doing it

Draw the shark here.

©1995 by Evan-Moor Corp.

Language Fundamentals

Super Sentence Challenge

Write each phrase after the question it answers to make a Super Sentence.

about 12:00

began to nibble a carrot

Gus

in the giant's garden

Who or What

Action

When

Where

Make a sentence out of the parts.
Use a capital letter at the beginning and a period at the end.

Super Sentence Challenge

Write each phrase after the question it answers to make a Super Sentence.

Bill's lunch pail
slithered out of
a few minutes ago
A snake

Who or What _____

Action _____

When _____

Where _____

Make a sentence out of the parts.
Use a capital letter at the beginning and a period at the end.

_____

_____

_____

_____

©1995 by Evan-Moor Corp. Language Fundamentals

Super Sentence Challenge

Write each phrase after the question it answers to make a Super Sentence.

after the sun set

The space creature

the little hill

peeked over

Who or What _____

Action _____

When _____

Where _____

Make a sentence out of the parts.
Use a capital letter at the beginning and a period at the end.

_____

_____

_____

_____

_____

_____

_____

_____

_____

Super Sentence Challenge

Write each phrase after the question it answers to make a Super Sentence.

danced around

at last night's show

the stage

The ballerina

Who or What _____

Action _____

When _____

Where _____

Make a sentence out of the parts.
Use a capital letter at the beginning and a period at the end.

_____

_____

_____

_____

_____

_____

Super Sentence Challenge

Write a phrase after the question to make a Super Sentence.

Who or What _____

Action _____

When _____

Where _____

Make a sentence out of the parts.
Use a capital letter at the beginning and a period at the end.

_____

_____

_____

_____

_____

Write Super Sentences

Choose words from each box to write as many Super Sentences about pigs as you can. You may also use words of your own. You will need to get some sheets of writing paper.

	describing words	who or what	did what?
The A Some Many All	chubby loveable famished pokey greedy	pig pigs piglet sow boar	gobbled its food scurried wallowed grunted noisily scratched

where?	when?
to the trough in the mud by the fence near the barn	many times each night at twilight before the farmer left at the fair

©1995 by Evan-Moor Corp. Language Fundamentals

Write Super Sentences

Choose words from each box to write as many Super Sentences about spaceships as you can. You may also use words of your own. You will need to get some sheets of writing paper.

	describing words	who or what	did what?
the	metallic	spaceship	approached
a	swift	vehicle	circled
many	graceful	transport	escaped
no	foreign	shuttle	ejected the equipment
suddenly	ancient	pod	encountered unusual
whenever	alien	module	life forms

where?	when?
a distant planet	after a long journey
around several asteroids	before landing
from gravity's pull	just in time
from inside the ship	after take-off
throughout the universe	during its explorations

©1995 by Evan-Moor Corp. Language Fundamentals

Paragraphs

- parts of a paragraph
- kinds of paragraphs
  - descriptive
  - direction
  - narrative
  - explanatory

Each kind of paragraph serves a different purpose:
Create word pictures (*descriptive paragraphs*).
Explain "how to" (*writing directions*).
Tell a story (*narrative*).
Explain to make something clear (*explanatory*).

Many children have difficulty with the concept of writing a paragraph that truly contains a main idea and supporting sentences. First and second graders need to be helped to write paragraphs that "make sense." By third grade you can begin to work on the elements of a paragraph. Page 208 contains activities to help with this process.

Page 210 contains a list of topic sentences you can use with students who have difficulty coming up with a topic. They can also be reproduced and placed in a writing center.

Provide experiences that help students recognize the topic of a paragraph.

1. Read sample paragraphs from literature or text books. Have children determine what the paragraph is about.

2. Read samples from children's own work. Have them determine if the topic is clear. (Put the paragraphs on overlays to use with a group of children.)

3. Practice arranging sentences in an order that makes sense. Select a paragraph. Put the sentences on tag strips. Have students work in small groups or independently to put the sentences in an order that forms a paragraph that makes sense. Begin with three sentences and work up to longer paragraphs. If your students are ready for a more difficult task, have them identify the topic sentence.

Pages 211-216 contain reproducible forms. You may need to do these as guided work with your students until they have had many writing experiences. Don't try to move them into independent work too quickly.

"What's the Big Idea?"

You need to lay some groundwork when your students are ready to write formal paragraphs. They need to understand the idea of "main idea" and "supporting details."

Use these sample paragraphs to practice locating both the topic or main idea sentence and the supporting details. You can write simple ones to use with beginners. You may use paragraphs from literature with older students. Use paragraphs from their own work also.

Put a paragraph on the chalkboard or on a plastic overlay. Help students read the paragraph. Ask them to give you the most important idea they see in the paragraph. Circle it.

> Ann takes good care of her pet cat. She keeps water in the cat's dish. She feeds him in the morning. She plays with her cat after school.

> Mr. Clark has an interesting job. He is a vet in a zoo. He gives shots to lions and elephants He gives them medicine when they are sick. He even has to operate on them sometimes.

> I carry out the garbage on Monday. I help my dad weed the garden. I make my bed and keep my bedroom tidy. I help my sister with the dinner dishes. Boy, do I have a lot of work to do!

"We Provide Support"

Put a paragraph on the chalkboard or on a plastic overlay. (See the sample paragraphs above.) Circle the main idea. Ask students to listen carefully as you read the paragraph again. Have them find the details that support the main idea. Underline them.

"What's My Topic Sentence?"

Use this oral activity to help children realize that there can be more than one appropriate topic sentence to fit a set of information.

Write these sets of information on a chart or on the chalkboard. Have each student select one group of details and write a topic (main idea) sentence that would work with the information. When everyone is finished, have students put their topic sentence by the set of information they chose. Go through each set to show the variety of topic sentences that students wrote.

Example:

facts:
warm sunshine
water
seeds
pull weeds

main idea sentences:
Your garden needs these things if it is going to grow.
Do you know what a garden needs to grow?
I wonder why my flowers didn't grow this year.

wash your face brush your teeth comb your hair get dressed hungry eat breakfast	built a nest laid eggs in the nest sat on the eggs gathered food for the babies
built a sand castle ran in and out of the waves explored the tide pools roasted hot dogs over a fire	gather ingredients spread peanut butter on bread put jelly on the bread too put the pieces together

Topic Sentences

Chocolate is my favorite flavor because....

- I love to eat _____ more than anything else in the world.

- I saw the strangest sight on the way to school today.

- Rain makes me feel _____ for these reasons.

- Did you ever notice how much _____ and _____are alike?

- _____ is the most exciting game to play.

- I have really changed since I was six. Then I... Now I...

- The worst book I ever read was _____.
  I didn't like it for these reasons.

- Let me explain how to _____. First...

- I had good reasons to feel _____. First...

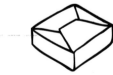

©1995 by Evan-Moor Corp.
Language Fundamentals

Cut and Paste a Paragraph

Make a paragraph about Ted and his fish.
Cut the sentences out.
Paste them in order to make a good paragraph.

Ted and His Fish

Paste the strips here.

He feeds them every day.

He keeps the cat away.

Ted takes good care of his pet fish.

He keeps the tank filled with fresh water.

©1995 by Evan-Moor Corp. Language Fundamentals

Note: Discuss the types of items that might turn up unexpectedly in a pocket. It could be a quarter you forgot about. It could be a tasty treat. It could a slimy surprise!

In My Pocket

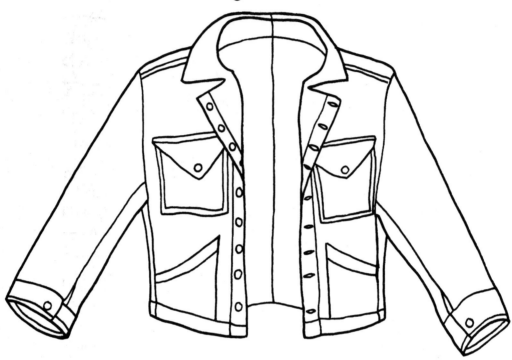

I had a big surprise when I put my hand in my jacket

pocket.   I found a _____ in it!
(Describe how it looks.)

_____

_____

(Describe how it feels.)

_____

_____

It makes me want to _____

_____

_____

©1995 by Evan-Moor Corp.   Language Fundamentals

Note: Brainstorm to make a list of ways we feel when an unexpected gift arrives on our doorsteps. Discuss ways we might try to take a "peek" to see what is inside the box.

I Can't Wait

Don't you hate it when a present comes for you and your mom says you have to wait to open it? Yesterday a huge surprise

came for me from my uncle. I felt _____

_____

_____

_____

_____

I think I'll _____

_____

_____

_____

_____

Draw the surprise.

Note: Discuss all the possible ways you can make a picture. What kinds of materials can you use (paint, pencil, torn paper, etc.)? What would the picture show? What steps would you follow to make it?

How to Create a Picture

CRAYON

I like to make pictures of _____

_____

First I _____

Second I _____

Third I _____

Last of all I _____

Draw a picture in each box to show what you did first, second, third, and last of all.

1	2
3	4

©1995 by Evan-Moor Corp.   Language Fundamentals

Sharks and Whales

Sharks and whales are alike in several ways. They both
_____
— — — — — — — — — — — — — — — — — — — —
_____
— — — — — — — — — — — — — — — —
They also — — — — — — — — — — — — — — — —
_____
— — — — — — — — — — — — — — — — — — — —
Finally _____

You can probably think of more ways they are alike.

Sharks and whales are different in several ways. A shark
_____   _____
— — — — — — — — — —   — — — — — — — — — —
_____ and   _____
_____   _____
— — — — — — — —   — — — — — — — — — —
A whale ——————————— and —————————

They are both interesting animals.

An Old Trunk

Fill in the blanks.

_____

Mark found an unusual _____ in an old trunk in

his grandmother's attic. He took it out and _____

He was surprised to find out _____

He decided to _____

Illustrate your paragraph.

Note: If your students are ready for independent writing, you may want to use this list to help them preparing their paragraphs. Put the points on a chart or give each child his/her own copy to use.

Writing a Paragraph

1. Choose a subject for your paragraph.

2. Think about what you want to tell in this paragraph. Write a topic sentence that gets the main idea across to your readers.

3. Add details to your paragraph. Each detail sentence should support the main idea.

4. Reread your paragraph. Can you see ways to change it to make it better?

5. Proof your paragraph.

___ I indented the first word.

___ I used correct punctuation marks.

___ The words are spelled correctly.

___ My paragraph says what I wanted it to say.

6. Copy your paragraph in your best handwriting.

©1995 by Evan-Moor Corp.

Language Fundamentals

Note: Here is a form third graders can use when they are writing a story or report requiring more than one paragraph.

Planning My Paragraphs

Select a subject. Write the most important things you want to say about it on lines 1, 2, and 3. These will become the main ideas for your paragraphs. Write supporting ideas on the other lines.

_____
subject

1. _____
main idea

   a. _____

   b. _____

   c. _____

2. _____
main idea

   a. _____

   b. _____

   c. _____

3. _____
main idea

   a. _____

   b. _____

   c. _____

Get a sheet of paper. Take these notes and use them as a guide as you write your paragraphs.

Stories

- parts of a story
- planning a story

How to Begin the Writing Process

Read many stories to your students. Include stories of different lengths, complexity, and genres. This will help build a strong background for students to draw from as they write their own stories.

Identify the parts of a story, helping students locate characters, setting, main plot points, and the conclusion. Begin with simple, short stories and move on to complex ones. Use some of your students' own stories as examples. Keep in mind your students' needs and skill level as you select stories. (Use the form on page 222 with older students. It provides a place to write about the different parts of any story they may read.)

Set Goals for yourself and for your students. Clearly communicate goals so students know whether a specific writing experience is for practice or if the goal is to complete a story to publish.

Model the writing process. Review the steps in the writing process you have been using with your students. If you have not been following a specific process, use this simple guide:

        Pre-writing - brainstorm, discuss possible topics and formats.
        Drafting - outline, rough draft
        Revising - receive responses from others, make changes
        Editing - proof grammar, punctuation, spelling, make final draft
        Publishing - illustrations, bind books, share with others

Monitor children's progress throughout the writing process. Be available to provide encouragement and ideas as they write. Invite students to serve as "editors" for one another also. This will provide another source of help and encouragement for them.

Provide Time and Materials that are appropriate for the purpose of the writing assignment.

"Publish" stories in some way. The revision process is the most difficult for children to use. You will need to do many modeling experiences. Start with short paragraphs. Use an overlay, where children can see the changes as you make them together. Guide them with your questions to improve clarity and interest by changing wording, adding details, removing unnecessary information, and rearranging the order of sentences/paragraphs. When children understand the process, divide them into pairs or small groups to respond to each other's work. It is important to set up guidelines and to have children practice appropriate responses.

©1995 by Evan-Moor Corp. Language Fundamentals

"Let's Tell a Story"

One of the best preparations for writing stories is hearing them and telling them. Spend some time every week telling stories to your class. Invite students to take turns telling stories of their own. These stories can be from "real life" or can be imaginary. Do a simple critique when the storyteller is through. Encourage positive reinforcement! "I liked the part where you rode your bike over the hill." "I wish you had told more about the lost kitten you found." "You make me want to meet your grandpa. He sounds nice."

"Making It Better"

Put a short paragraph on the chalkboard or on an overlay. Make it very simple. Leave out a detail or two. You may want to include a sentence of extraneous material. Read it with your students. Then ask them a series of questions to help them rewrite the paragraph in a more interesting and complete way.

- Do you see a sentence that does not belong in this paragraph?
- Can you think of a detail that makes the main idea clearer?
- What adjectives can we add to make this sentence more interesting/clearer?
- Is there a better way to arrange these sentences?

"The Edit Squad"

Do this activity on the chalkboard using colored chalk for the editing task or use plastic overlays and erasable pens. Start with simple sentences with beginning writers and work up to paragraphs with older, more experienced students.

Have students read the incorrect sentence, then copy it on their individual chalkboards or a sheet of paper, making any corrections. (If you are doing paragraphs, you may want to reproduce the material so it won't be so time-consuming.) When students are finished, call up one child at a time to mark an error and make the correction.

Have your students use proofreader's marks if these have been introduced. If not, have students locate errors and mark them out with colored chalk or pens. Discuss what should be used to replace the mistake.

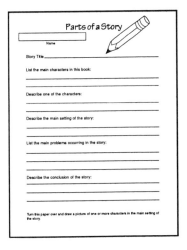

Writing a Story

Recognizing Parts of a Story:
Pages 222-226 provide practice in identifying and writing about characters, setting, problems/plot, and solutions/conclusions. Do these as guided activities or as independent work.

Planning a Story:
Pages 227-228 provide a story checklist and a story plan sheet. The checklist helps the young writer keep track of what needs to be done. The story plan sheet helps students begin the writing process by thinking about the whole story, so they have a definite direction as they write.

Model the process for using each form. Make a copy of each form on a plastic overlay or write it on the chalkboard. Reproduce copies of the checklist for each child to use. Work through planning a story using a topic of interest to your students. Fill in each area as you plan the story together. Leave the plan sheet where everyone can see it as they write a story. Have them complete the checklist as they do each step.

When you feel students are ready for independent story writing, provide planning and check sheets and set them to creating!

Pages 229-230 contain other forms which can be used to plan a story.

©1995 by Evan-Moor Corp.

Language Fundamentals

Parts of a Story

Name

Story Title _____

List the main characters in this book:

_____

_____

Describe one of the characters:

_____

_____

Describe the main setting of the story:

_____

_____

List the main problems occurring in the story:

_____

_____

_____

Describe the conclusion of the story:

_____

_____

_____

Turn this paper over and draw a picture of one or more characters in the main setting of the story.

Describing the Characters

Underline the words and phrases that describe these characters.

in a dark corner of the room	a loud creaking sound
watching in suspense	wagging tail
running around in circles	strange
brave	jumping up and down
bent over	a wise smile on his face
curious	trees bending in the wind
freckled face	bright moon shining through
scratched and dented	

Write a paragraph using some of the descriptive words and phrases you underlined to introduce these characters to your reader.

_____

_____

_____

_____

_____

_____

Describing the Setting

Underline the words and phrases that describe this setting.

tall trees waving in the wind	timid deer looking around
colorful flowers scattered around	birds flying overhead
field of green grass	merry sound of birds singing
rain falling from the sky	warm sun shining
bats flying among the trees	fish jumping out of the river
rabbits hopping across the field	sand dunes
sun setting behind the clouds	giraffe nibbling leaves

Using the words and phrases you underlined, write a paragraph describing
the setting to your readers.

_____

_____

_____

_____

_____

_____

_____

Describing Story Problems

Underline the words and phrases that describe the
problem shown in this picture.

hungry bear	injured leg
trapped in a cave	crying for help
broken wheel on the bike	a bad accident
rain pouring down	helicopter flying overhead
thunder and lightning	policeman down the street
far from home	attacked by bees
no one passing by	

Arrange the words and phrases you underlined in logical order and write
a paragraph describing the main story problems.

_____

_____

_____

_____

_____

_____

_____

Writing a Conclusion

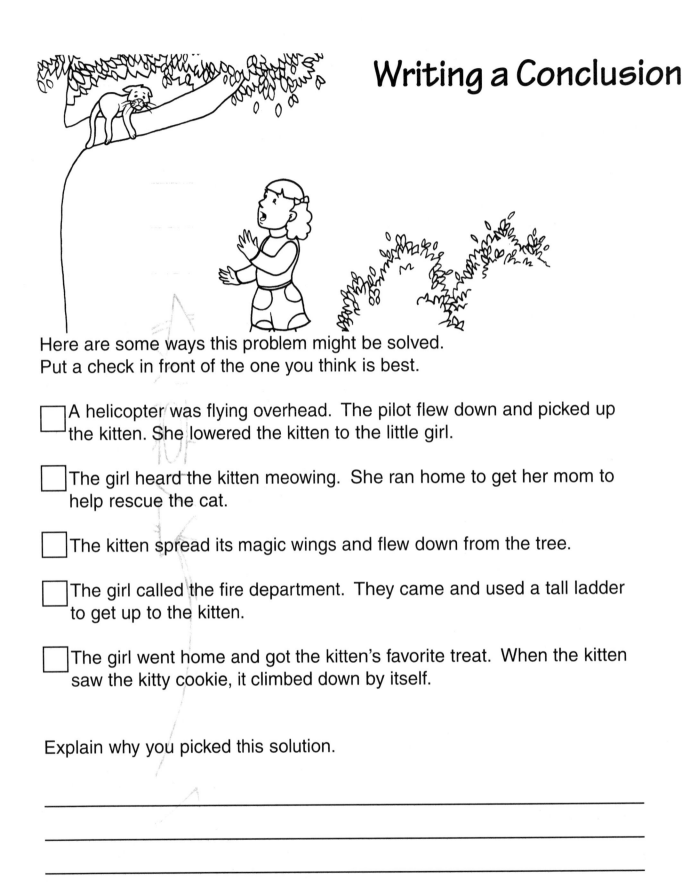

Here are some ways this problem might be solved.
Put a check in front of the one you think is best.

☐ A helicopter was flying overhead. The pilot flew down and picked up the kitten. She lowered the kitten to the little girl.

☐ The girl heard the kitten meowing. She ran home to get her mom to help rescue the cat.

☐ The kitten spread its magic wings and flew down from the tree.

☐ The girl called the fire department. They came and used a tall ladder to get up to the kitten.

☐ The girl went home and got the kitten's favorite treat. When the kitten saw the kitty cookie, it climbed down by itself.

Explain why you picked this solution.

_____

_____

_____

_____

Now write a different solution to the same problem,
using your own imagination.

©1995 by Evan-Moor Corp. Language Fundamentals

Story Checklist

☐ **1.** Before you begin, decide on...

  • type of story (realistic, fantasy) _____

  • main idea for plot (problem) _____

  • main location and time period (setting)_____

☐ **2.** Write the story

  rough draft _____

  revise story _____

  edit story _____

      content
      _____ language

      _____ story order

      _____ conclusion

      mechanics
      _____ spelling

      _____ punctuation

      _____ final copy made

☐ **3.** Illustrate the story

☐ **4.** Make a cover

☐ **5.** Share the story with others

Story Plan Sheet

Character
Who

_____

_____

_____

_____

Setting
Where

_____

_____

_____

_____

Plot
What happened and why?

1. _____

_____

_____

2. _____

_____

_____

3. _____

_____

_____

Conclusion
The End

_____

_____

5 Ws and an H

Who? _____

Did what? _____

Where? _____

When? _____

Why? _____

How? _____

_____

_____

Sequence and Write

Draw a picture for each part of your story.	Write a paragraph about each picture.

beginning

middle

end

_____
_____
_____
_____
_____
_____
_____
_____
_____
_____
_____
_____
_____
_____
_____
_____
_____
_____
_____
_____
_____
_____
_____
_____
_____

Editing

- editing checklist
- introduction to proofreader's marks

It is important to have children write, write, write. Beginning writers need to be concerned with the flow of ideas and the process of getting them on paper. In the beginning don't worry about mechanics as much as about content.

Once you decide your students are ready to do some editing and correcting, plan how much you expect them to do. You may set a goal of checking for capital letters and periods for one writing experience. Another day you may have students check for correct spelling in a story.

When your students have had a lot of practice in writing, you may have them begin to do a complete editing for content and mechanics. Page 232 contains a final checklist.

By third grade many students are ready to begin recognizing and using proofreader's marks. Introduce the marks slowly, giving students plenty of time to become comfortable with what the marks mean. Pages 233-235 provide practice with these six marks.

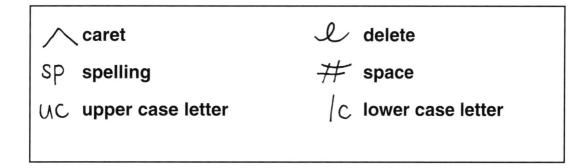

∧ **caret**	ℓ **delete**
SP **spelling**	# **space**
UC **upper case letter**	/c **lower case letter**

My Final Check

Content:

☐ My story is in the correct order.

☐ My language is clear.

☐ My ending makes sense.

Mechanics:

☐ I spelled the words correctly.

☐ I used capital letters in the right places.

☐ I used punctuation marks where they were needed.

Final Copy:

☐ I copied my story carefully.

☐ I used good handwriting.

Reading Proofreader's Marks

Match:

caret   *e*

delete   ∧

spelling   lc

upper case   #

lower case   sp

space   uc

Reading Proofreader's Marks

Mark this paragraph with proofreader's marks.

A very strange plant grows in North Carolina. it eats insects? It has leaves that wurk like a steeltrap. The two halves of the the leaf are hinged in the middle. Wen an insect lands on if, the leaf closes and traps the insect the plant uses the soft parts of The insect as food.

Copy this paragraph.
Make the corrections.

_____

_____

_____

_____

_____

_____

_____

_____

Using Proofreader's Marks

Find the mistakes in these sentences.
Use proofreader's marks.
Put the marks in the left margin.

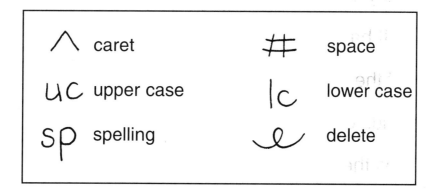

∧ caret	# space
UC upper case	lc lower case
SP spelling	ℓ delete

1. mike wanted to make kookies.

2. Mike got oatmeal eggs, and milk.

3. He broke the eggsand poured the milk into a big bowl.

4. Dad came home and found Mike making kookies.

5. "Wait a minute, son." sed Dad.

6. Dad helped Mike Read the recipe.

7. they each ate three cookies before dinner.

8. All of of the cookies were gone.

Publishing

- group and individual books
- illustrations
- covers for stories

One of the most rewarding aspects of writing an interesting story is watching someone else read and enjoy it. Publishing can be as simple as binding special stories into books for a special event or as complex as running an on-going publishing center in your classroom. In either case, it is worth it!

Group Books

These books can be done by the whole class, a smaller reading group, or a few students with an interest in common. Have each person in the group create a page or more to go in the book. Select (or have the group select) someone to make the cover. Bind the book and put it in an accessible place for everyone to enjoy. Try alphabet books, counting books, books on a common theme (animals, giants, etc.), or retell familiar fairy tales.

Individual Books

Plan to spend quite a bit of time for children to create individual books. They need plenty of time to create, write, illustrate, and bind their books. You may have everyone working on the same theme or have each child select his/her own topic. Move among your eager authors, providing encouragement and help as they work through the whole process.

Illustrations

Spend some time sharing illustrations in your students favorite books. Point out the different techniques and materials used (paint, pencil, collage, printing, etc.) and the various places illustrations have been located. Provide a variety of types of paper and art materials for children to use in illustrating their stories. Here are some materials you might like to try.

crayons	marking pens
colored pencils	water colors
paper bags	wallpaper samples
print-making materials	ink pens
construction paper	newspaper

Encourage students to try interesting arrangements of words and pictures.

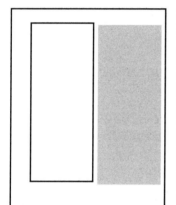  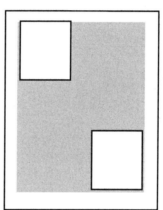 

Special Pages

Enhance your books by adding pages such as these to both group and individual books.

1. Title Page
Include the title, author, illustrator, room number, and school.

2. Dedication Page
Dedicate the story to someone special or to someone who was especially helpful in writing the story.

3. About the Author
Have the authors describe themselves, including likes, dislikes, and special interests. Have them explain why they chose the subject of their stories. Invite them to include a school photograph if one is available or draw a self-portrait.

Bind the Story

Book-binding can be as simple as stapling a story between two sheets of construction paper. However, if you and your students have taken the time to carefully write a story, you may want to make a more special binding for it. If you are fortunate enough to have a binding machine available, you can make a very professional-looking book quickly. If not, here are a few ideas you can try.

1. Put the Book Together
Have students follow this sequence to put their story pages in order.

2. Attach Story Pages
Pages may be stapled together before being put into a cover.

Pages may be glued to a backing of construction paper, newspaper,or brown paper from a grocery bag, then stapled together and put into a cover.

Pages may be folded in half and stitched down the center. Stitching can be done on a machine (by an adult) or by hand with darning needles.

3. Make a Cover
Follow the directions on page 239 for "quick and easy covers" ..

mat board	tagboard	cardboard
construction paper	cloth	Con-Tact paper
wallpaper	wrapping paper	newspaper
brown paper bags	cellophane tape	masking tape
cloth tape	duct tape	stapler

Always cut cover pieces 1/4 to 1/2 inch (.6 - 1.25 centimeters) larger than the writing paper.

Quick and Easy Covers

These covers require little time to create.

1. Staple cover to story pages.
Cover the staples with a strip of tape.

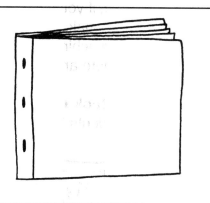

2. Punch holes through the cover and story pages.
Put the book together with metal rings.

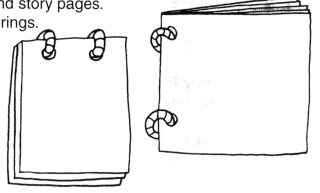

3. Punch holes through the cover and story pages.
Tie the book together with shoe laces, yarn, or sturdy string.

a. down through the holes   b. up through middle hole   c. tie on top

Answer Key
Part Four

Page 200
who-Gus
action-began to nibble
when-about 12:00
where-in the giant's garden

Page 201
who-A snake
action-slithered out of
when-a few minutes ago
where-Bill's lunch pail

Page 202
who-The space creature
action-peeked over
when-after the sunset
where-the little hill

Page 203
who-The ballerina
action-danced around
when-at last night's show
where-the stage

Page 211
Answers will vary.

Page 223
Answers may vary

Page 224
Answers may vary.

Page 225
Answers may vary.

Page 234
See Proofreader's Chart on page 233 for markings.
A very strange plant grows in North Carolina. It eats insects! It has leaves that work like a steel trap. The two halves of the leaf are hinged in the middle. When an insect lands on it, the leaf closes and traps the insect. The plant uses the soft parts of the insect as food.

Page 235
See Proofreader's Chart on page 233 for markings.
1. Mike wanted to make cookies.
2. Mike got oatmeal, eggs, and milk.
3. He broke the eggs and poured the milk into a big bowl.
4. Dad came home and found Mike making cookies.
5. "Wait a minute, son." said Dad
6. Dad helped Mike read the recipe.
7. They each ate three cookies before dinner.
8. All of the cookies were gone.